SADE MY NEIGHBOR

Northwestern University
Studies in Phenomenology
and
Existential Philosophy

Translated and with an Introduction by

Alphonso Lingis

SADE MY NEIGHBOR

Pierre Klossowski

Northwestern University Press
Evanston, Illinois

1991

Northwestern University Press
Evanston, Illinois 60201

First published in French as *Sade mon prochain* by Editions du Seuil,
Paris. Copyright © 1947, 1967 by Editions du Seuil. English translation
published 1991 by arrangement with Editions du Seuil. Copyright ©
1991 by Northwestern University Press. All rights reserved.
First published 1991 by Northwestern University Press

Printed in the United States of America

97 96 95 94 93 92 91   7 6 5 4 3 2 1

Library of Congress Cataloging-in-Publication Data

Klossowski, Pierre.
    [Sade mon prochain. English]
    Sade my neighbor / Pierre Klossowski ; translated and with an
introduction by Alphonso Lingis.
        p.   cm. — (Northwestern University studies in phenomenology
and existential philosophy)
    Translation of: Sade mon prochain.
    Includes bibliographical references.
    ISBN 0-8101-0957-3 (hard : alk. paper). — ISBN 0-8101-0958-1
(pbk. : alk. paper)
    1. Sade, marquis de, 1740–1814—Criticism and interpretation.
2. Sade, marquis de, 1740–1814—Philosophy.   3. Erotic literature,
French—History and criticism.   4. Philosophy in literature.
I. Title.   II. Series: Northwestern University studies in
phenomenology & existential philosophy.
PQ2063.S3K513   1991
843'.6—dc20   90-25362
                                                          CIP

The paper used in this publication meets the minimum requirements of
American National Standard for Information Sciences—Permanence of
Paper for Printed Library Materials, ANSI Z39.48-1984

Contents

Translator's Introduction

Not only did the Second World War confront European thinkers with the refutation of their progressivist, liberationist Enlightenment understanding of technological development; the extremities of gratuitous cruelty and of the self-destruction of European industries and nations seemed to confront Europeans with *the unthinkable*. The notion or anti-notion of the absurd seemed henceforth an essential category of philosophy. Philosophers of history were returned to the center of study, philosophers whose history proceeded by contradictions—although now the contradictions did not inevitably result in the advance of the spirit. The ancient category of tragedy came to be seen as an essential category of history. Psychoanalysis seemed relevant inasmuch as it posited an unsurpassable infantilism in the structure of the human psyche.

There was one figure in recent European history whose eighteenth-century imagination had preceded the twentieth century in the resolution to go all the way into brutality and viciousness, one who deliberately wrote a literature that, Blanchot said, could be allowed in no conceivable social order. This figure is the Marquis de Sade. The manuscript and, Sade believed, all copies of his magnum opus, *The 120 Days of Sodom*, written during his long imprisonment in the Bastille, were destroyed in his own lifetime (a copy was found in Germany in this century); after his death all copies found of his work were burned by his family; and his descendants continued to make sure that publication of any of his writings that had nonetheless survived was forbidden in France until the end of the 1950s. Now, after

World War II, thinkers began to turn to his work in a desperate effort to understand the nightmares the European Enlightenment seemed to have engendered. Sade's work, of unsurpassable monstrosity, is, paradoxically, rationalist in construction, even hyperrationalist, a Leibnitzian *mathesis universalis* of evil, and pedagogic in genre. Is Sade then *thinkable*? Does his importance for a Europe mourning the devastation of its populations and its rational programs lie in the demonstration Sade undertakes of how a rationalism, a hyperrationalism, comprehends and embraces the last limits of evil? Or is it that under the form of rationalism something else—seduction and contamination—is at work in this writing; or rather that in his writing the form of rationalism itself becomes seduction and contamination?

In writing below the title of his *Philosophy in the Bedroom*, "Mothers will give this to their daughters," Sade indicated sardonically that this book was the realization of his dream of writing a work that, although apparently appealing to the rational faculty in his reader in order to persuade, would instead infect, contaminate, such that were it universally banned, as it must be in every society formed by contract, it would be enough for it to exist, and one day someone would come upon it, and it would be enough for that someone to open its pages to be damned. Today we are appalled to see that the progress of our scientific enlightenment has now stockpiled on our planet a nuclear arsenal capable of annihilating a Hiroshima-sized city every day for the next 550 years. With our reason we have delivered into our hands the power to consign the whole of our species to extinction—indeed to annihilate definitively all life on this, the sole planet upon which life is known to exist. This power is not only the final and fullest extension of every cruelty and viciousness, it is the power to annihilate every possibility of every cruelty and viciousness; it is the power to annihilate every possibility of justification or condemnation. We have also come to recognize, to our horror, that if the existing arsenal should be destroyed through international agreement, and all the industries capable of manufacturing such weapons dismantled, and all the blueprints for such industries burned, the power to re-create them, the power to bring extinction upon the species, could never be extirpated from the planet as long as the fundamental principles of rational science are at large in the minds of men. In the reasons with which we allowed ourselves to be persuaded of those principles was there not from the first a clandestine force of seduction at work, by which the terminal power of the absolutely antihuman came to infect irradicably all our human forces? Henceforth in every society formed by contract, when we falter and look to our brother, is it not Sade we see?

Pierre Klossowski was the first philosopher in war-torn France to set out to penetrate the blackness of Sade's work, a task more demanding than that of penetrating the obscurities of Kant and Hegel. In this succinct study, *Sade My Neighbor*, now translated into English, Klossowski tracked down what is most singular in Sade's enormous body of writing: a philosophy of Nature in perpetual motion which is neither innocent nor neutral with regard to evil; a theology of supreme evil and a depraved anthropology centered on the figures of the hermaphrodite virgin and the sodomite; an ethics of an imperative to outrage and of mastery as integral monstrosity; a psychoanalysis of the negative Oedipus complex; and a semiotics of the black holes in the integral rationalism in which all this is elaborated. Small wonder, then, that this book has been one of the sources of some of the most original work in France for the past forty years.

To be sure, Sade's reason is aberrant, enslaved to evil passions. The Enlightenment had believed that the discursive movements of reason were also the advances of freedom, that the conclusions of reason were also the constructive achievements of the good, that freedom was *virtù* and virtue was freedom. The rise of a specifically technological reason showed a reason that was value-free, indifferent with regard to virtue and vice, with regard to freedom and slavery. Indeed, the juggernaut of technological war seemed to suggest to thinkers like Heidegger that technological reason was intrinsically alien to every human purpose and finality, intrinsically alien to and destructive of every finality. The idea then that Sade's reason, aberrant and prostituted to evil passions as it is, is nonetheless reason could be taken seriously. Klossowski set out to disengage in Sade's writings, even in the literary works, all constructed as pedagogical demonstrations, the *rational system*.

If, certainly, the intellectual anxiety of war-ravaged Europe was the motivating context for taking up the serious study of Sade's writings, the intention to illuminate the present conjuncture by these writings would require one to examine them in their own social context, that of the Enlightened hopes, and terror, of the French Revolution. Klossowski proceeds to show how the passions of revolution, which *les philosophes* saw as a grand experiment aimed at liberating natural man and making his norms rule, could also give rise to men, such as Sade, who see in social upheavals the chance to repudiate natural man entirely.

Natural man is the one who is normalized, that is, whose constituent organs function for the integrity of the whole, and whose individual integrity functions for the maintenance and reproduction of the species. The species integrity, the imperative for the maintenance and reproduction of the species, would be the corporeal basis in each individual for every communication and every norm, and in particular for the rational form of communication and rational norms.

Sade's rationalism is atheist, even anti-theist. It is not so much a disavowal of God as a sustained assault on God. God would be the ultimate formula for norms. God then would be the counterpart of the realm of the general and the generic, the realm of the species, the imperative of the species in the individual. God would be the formula for the integrity of natural man, species man, in the individual.

Sadean rationalism would then be the project of formulating a new reason that would repudiate natural man, generic man, and the God corresponding to him. It would be the project of using the medium of the generality, of the generic, to undermine generic man and promote the singular case, the monster.

The first essay in *Sade My Neighbor* is in fact the last to have been composed,[1] and it carries Klossowski's thought the furthest. In "The Philosopher-Villain" Klossowski sets out to show how in Sade rational language formulates a sign of the destruction of generic signs and norms. The *mathesis universalis* of the total combinatorium of simple and compound passions which Sade elaborated in *The 120 Days of Sodom* is generated about the key sign of sodomy. Sodomy is not simply anal eroticism, a natural and animal pleasure; it is anal eroticism biblically and theologically interpreted as an act that functions neither for the reproduction of the species nor for species bonding, as an act done to gore the partner and release the germ of the species in his excrement. Thus sodomy, theologically interpreted, is an assault on the human species as such, an act of monstrous singularity, and an act directed against God, the ultimate formula for all norms.

The libertine, in his sodomite perversion, is the materialization of the theological sign of sodomy, a sign within rational discourse of the destruction of the generic substrate for all generality. The project for such libertinage could be formulated—indeed could only be formulated—in the medium of rationalist discourse. Klossowski shows that rational discourse contains the intrinsic possibility of such a sign, such a black hole in the medium of discourse. Rationalism itself, then, contains the possibility of such a rationalist project of the destruction of natural man, of the human species as such.

Could it be that such a rationalism is in effect not only in the banned writings of Sade but in the history writ large of our time of holocaust and thermonuclear extinction? Does rationalism, which elaborates signs to affirm and normalize all things, of itself engender vertiginous signs in which the material substrates of norms are annihilated? And what is the specific force of attraction of these vertiginous signs? What light does the splendor of the Sadean great libertines throw on every rational project of individual sovereignty?

Some of the most influential thinkers of France were persuaded of the exceptional importance of Klossowski's work. Simone de Beauvoir and Maurice Blanchot wrote of the importance of an understanding of Sade for political theory; Georges Bataille and Klossowski himself wrote about the importance of Sade for sociology. Jacques Lacan took repeated account of Klossowski's work in his reconstruction of psychoanalytic theory; Gilles Deleuze wrote a work to disengage the specific structures of masochism and show it to be not simply the counterpart to sadism. Not only was Klossowski's book the origin of all this literature on sadist rationality and sadism in rationalism, but it has proved to be a permanent and fundamental source of political, sociological, and psychoanalytic thinking in our time.

Born in 1905 of an old Polish line, the counts Klossowski de Rola, Pierre Klossowski knew André Gide, Pierre Bonnard, and Rainer Maria Rilke from boyhood. He entered a seminary of the Dominican order but left before ordination. He acted in films directed by Bresson. He did not pursue a university career and relied mainly on translation for income. His wife, Denise, is the central figure of his novels as well as of his art, which consists of large-format pencil drawings. His brother is the celebrated painter Balthus.

Klossowski went on to publish fundamental works on Nietzsche: his *Nietzsche ou le cercle vicieux* is recognized as the most important work on Nietzsche published since

Heidegger's. Unlike Heidegger's interpretation, which reinscribes Nietzsche in the evolution of metaphysical concepts, Klossowski's brings out in Nietzsche all that is radically outside the metaphysical categoreal system. Earlier Klossowski had published a series of writings on, and translations of, authors from Greek and Roman classicism. His other principal theoretical works are *Un si funeste désir* (1963), *La monnaie vivante* (1970), and *La ressemblance* (1984). His distinctive, and likewise influential, novels include *Roberte ce soir* (1954), *La révocation de l'édit de Nantes* (1959), *Le souffleur* (1960), and *Le Baphomet* (1965). He has also translated into French Virgil, Hölderlin, Paul Klee, Kafka, Heidegger, Wittgenstein, and Nietzsche.

—Alphonso Lingis

SADE MY NEIGHBOR

For Pierre Leyris

ROBERTE: Who gave Antoine that book he was reading last night? Was it you, or did Victor already pass it on to him? The title alone is enough to make one vomit: "Sade My Neighbor"!

OCTAVE: Make who vomit?

ROBERTE: Every self-respecting atheist! As far as your Sade is concerned, I am happy to leave him to you. But to use him to try to convince us that one cannot be an atheist without being at the same time a pervert! The pervert insults God in order to make him exist; he then believes in him! This would be the proof that he secretly cherishes God! In that way one tries to make the unbeliever disgusted with his sane conviction. . . .

—*Roberte ce soir*

Preface

In distancing myself from the state of mind that made me write, "Sade *my neighbor*," I do not find myself any closer to those who have always taken Sade's atheism to be fundamental, and as a proof of the liberating force of a liberated thought. Liberated from God—whom atheism declares to be nothing—had this thought then liberated itself from nothing? Would its freedom also be for . . . nothing?

The recently composed study "The Philosopher-Villain" sets out to answer this question. Placed first in this new edition of an older work, its task is not only to note revisions of the author's first conception but also, if possible, to fill a serious lacuna. Had the author persevered in his original design, which he had begun to work out in the "Outline of Sade's System"—the oldest of the studies collected in this book—perhaps he would at that time have pursued a more rigorous examination of Sade's relationship with reason, on the basis of the following observations: (1) Rational atheism is the heir to monotheist norms, upholding a unitary economy of the soul, along with the possession and identity of a responsible ego. (2) If the sovereignty of man is the principle and the goal of rational atheism, Sade, liquidating the norms of reason, pursues the disintegration of man. (3) In the absence of any conceptual formulation other than that of the rational materialism of his age (as the "Outline" already notes), Sade made of atheism the "religion" of integral monstrosity. (4) This "religion" involves an asceticism, that of the apathetic reiteration of acts, which confirms the insufficiency of atheism. (5) Through this asceticism, Sade's atheism reintroduces a divine character in monstrosity, divine in the sense that its "real presence" is actualized only through rites, that is, reiterated acts. (6). Thus it turns out that it is not atheism that conditions or liberates Sadean monstrosity; rather, this monstrosity leads Sade to derationalize atheism as soon as he tries to rationalize his own monstrosity by way of atheism.

To describe Sade's thought is one thing; to describe Sade's sadism is another. It would have been necessary to recognize the irreducible, primitive fact of sodomy, from which sterile pleasure taken in a sterile object, experienced as a simulacrum of the destruction of norms, develops the Sadean emotion. Then one could show that under the cover of a rational signification, it is an affective aberration that denounces the one God, guarantor of the norms, as an aberration of reason. This denunciation is, in accordance with a law of thought itself, inscribed in a circuit of complicity. Can thought ever break such a circuit?

But instead of following the path opened up by the "Outline of Sade's System," the author confused his subject by taking it into his head to prolong this first study with analytic reflections concerning Sade's soul, using the psycho-theological schema of an absolute desire determined by the absolute object (God, the depth of the soul). The last part of the work ("Under the Mask of Atheism") now seems to the author to plunge the issue into a quasi-Wagnerian romanticism. Under the pretext of describing something like an "unhappy consciousness" in Sade, it ends up attributing sadism to unbelief. It does so through argumentation that is in itself perfectly coherent: the signification that Sade's mind ascribes to itself is constructed on the basis of an interdiction; by censoring God, this mind strikes, in the absolute object, against the absolute desire; but it does not thereby strike down the persistence of this desire. For the desire is here the repudiated immortality in which Sade's mind can no longer recognize itself, but which it henceforth experiences in the extent of its distress. With this interdiction against "believing in God," which Sade puts on himself and takes to be a rational signification, the Sadean ego breaks up its own wholeness; there results a perpetual and reciprocal transgression of desire by the mind—which can maintain this signification only if it determines to destroy this object—and of the mind by desire—which persists in attaching itself to this object. Out of this discordant simultaneity there would arise in Sade's mind the confounding, in one and the same demand, of the purification of desire with the destruction of its object, where the destruction is voluptuous only inasmuch as the voluptuousness derives from the wounded desire and covers over the soul's vexation over the loss of the absolute object.

It was no doubt the intention to free Sade from the narrow limits of a rational commentary that led the author to elucidate the Sadean experience, such as the author then conceived it, in terms of the longing for incorporeal purity in the Manichaean gnosis of Marcion, and to find in sadist behavior an analogue of the Carpocratian cult of orgasm, taken to liberate the "heavenly light." But this reference to the heresiarchs would have been truly clarifying only if the author had kept his distance from all representations, and particularly those of orthodox dogmatism. Then he would not have represented or imagined Sade's "unhappy consciousness" in the light of a "courtly"—but more a "clerical"—apologia of virginity, as he irremediably did so represent it in the chapter "Homage to the Virgin"; nor would he have explained this "unhappiness" as a complex of virility faced with the paradoxical image of the Virgin. He did not see that this image, inasmuch as it signifies the death of the procreative instinct, is a (monotheist) normalization of the myth of the androgynous one. The author conjured away the motif of sodomy—which is fundamental in Sade—dissimulating it under the theme of a virility accursed in its aspiration to possess the unpossessable virgin,[1] who is an incarnation of heavenly purity, and proposed this as the wellspring of Sade's psychological makeup. Such is the romanticism in which the author confesses he indulged at the time, but whose pious intention he must today reject.

THE
PHILOSOPHER—
VILLAIN

I t will be our task here to envision Sade's experience as it was conveyed in writing.[1] First, we shall try to define the philosophical position he took, or made a pretense of taking, in his novels.

The question will be: What do thinking and writing—as opposed to feeling or acting—mean for Sade?

Sade himself, so as to definitively disavow authorship of his *Justine*, declares that all the "philosophers" in his "own" works are "decent people," whereas "through an inexcusable clumsiness that was bound to set the author [of *Justine*] at loggerheads with wise men and fools alike," "all the philosophical characters in this novel are villains to the core."[2]

The confrontation of the philosopher–decent man with the philosopher-villain dates from Plato. The philosopher–decent man sets forth the act of thinking as the sole valid activity of his being. The villain who philosophizes grants thought only the value of favoring the activity of the strongest passion—which in the eyes of the decent man is and always will be only a lack of being. If the summit of villainy consists in disguising one's passion as thought, the villain for his part finds in the thought of a decent man nothing but the disguise of an impotent passion.

To do Sade justice, we should have to take this "villainous philosophy" seriously. Laid out in a vast work, it puts a sinister question mark on the decision to think and to write—particularly to think of and describe an act instead of committing it.

This decision does not resolve the dilemma: how can one give an account of an irreducible depth of sensibility except by acts that betray it? It would seem that such an irreducible depth can never be reflected on or grasped save by acts perpetrated outside of thought—unreflected and ungraspable acts.

The Act of Writing in Sade

The peculiarly human act of writing presupposes a generality that a singular case claims to join, and by belonging to this generality claims to come to understand itself. Sade as a singular case conceives his act of writing as verifying such belongingness. The medium of generality in Sade's time is the logically structured language of the classical tradition; in its structure this language reproduces and reconstitutes in the field of communicative gestures the normative structure of the human race in individuals. This normative structure is expressed physiologically by a subordination of the life functions, a subordination that ensures the preservation and propagation of the race. To this need to reproduce and perpetuate oneself which is in force in each individual there corresponds the need to reproduce and perpetuate oneself by language. Whence the reciprocity of persuasion, which makes possible the exchange of individual singularities in the circuit of generality. This reciprocity is brought about only in conformity with the principle of identity or of noncontradiction, which makes logically structured language one with the general principle of understanding, that is, universal reason.

With this principle of the normative generality of the human race in mind, Sade sets out to establish a countergenerality that would obtain for the specificity of perversions, making exchange between singular cases of perversion possible. These, in the existing normative generality, are defined by the absence of logical structure. Thus is conceived Sade's notion of integral monstrosity.

Sade takes this countergenerality, valid for the specificity of perversion, to be already implicit in the existing generality. For he thinks that the atheism proclaimed by normative reason, in the name of man's freedom and sovereignty, is destined to reverse the existing generality into this countergenerality. Atheism, the supreme act of normative reason, is thus destined to establish the reign of the total absence of norms.

In choosing as a testimony of that act of reason which is atheism the perverse way of feeling and acting, devoid of logic, Sade immediately puts universal reason into question; he makes it contradict itself by being applied. And he puts into question human behavior inasmuch as it proceeds from the subordination of the life functions.

Sade's Critique of Atheism

How does reason arrive at atheism? By deciding that the notion of God would still alter reason's autonomy in an illogical, hence monstrous, direction. It declares that from the notion of God, which is arbitrary in itself, all arbitrary, perverse and monstrous behavior derives. If atheism can prevail as a decision of autonomous reason, it is because this autonomy claims that it itself alone maintains the norms of the species in the individual and ensures behavior in humans in conformity with these norms, through the subordination of the life functions in each for the equality and freedom of all. How could autonomous reason include phenomena contrary to the preservation of the species and foreign to its own structure without the very concept of autonomous reason being altered? But Sade does change its concept, by working out, if only implicitly, a critique of normative reason. For Sade this atheism is still nothing but an inverted monotheism, only apparently purified of idolatry and scarcely distinguishable from deism. Just as the deist certified the notion of God, this atheism stands as a guarantee of the responsible ego, its possession and individual identity. For atheism to be purified of this inverted monotheism, it must become integral. What then will become of human behavior? One thinks that Sade will answer: See my monsters. And no doubt he himself shuffled the cards sufficiently for one to suppose him capable of giving so naive an answer.

In expressing himself in accordance with the concepts of universal reason, Sade can never account for the positive content of perversion, the polymorphous sensibility, other than with negative concepts that derive from this reason. Thus, while situating himself on the diametrically opposite side from the "tonsured henchmen," he cannot avoid the reprobation of right-thinking atheists, who will never forgive him for having, through the detour of atheism, rejoined the monstrosity of divine arbitrariness. Reason would like to be wholly freed of God. Sade—but in a very underhanded way— wishes to free thought from all preestablished normative reason: integral atheism will be the end of anthropomorphic reason. Although this obscure will is at work in him, Sade does not, and does not seek to, distinguish the act of thinking from the act of referring to the universal reason hypostatized in his concept of nature. This distinction is expressed only in the aberrant acts he describes; thought here ranges over an experimental field. Whether through heedlessness, or out of malicious pleasure taken in contradictory situations, in his novels he gives his characters the aspect of "philosophers who are villains to the core."

If these characters refer their anomalous acts to normative reason, they do so in a way that lays waste the autonomy of reason. They deride and demonstrate the vanity of a reason that, in its supreme act, atheism, claims to guarantee human forms of behavior. Unless atheism is reconceived on the basis of phenomena that reason rejects, it will continue to consolidate the existing institutions based on anthropomorphic norms. One then has this dilemma: either reason itself is excluded from its autonomous decision—atheism—which is to forestall monstrosity in man, or else monstrosity is once again removed from all possible argumentation.

Sade's Description of the Sadean Experience

The description Sade gives of his own experience in the characters he created covers a twofold experimentation: (1) that of the representation of the sensuous in an aberrant act; (2) that of the described representation.

There will then be a relationship between the actualization of the sensuous in an act through writing and the performing of the act independently of its description.

With Sade, this writing is not purely descriptive (objective) but interpretive. In interpreting the aberrant act as a coinciding of sensuous nature with reason, Sade humiliates reason with sensuous nature and humiliates the "rational" sensuous nature with a perverse reason. The perverse reason is nonetheless the counterpart to the reason that censors sensuous nature. As such, perverse reason retains the censorship and introduces into the "rational" sensuous nature punitive sanction as an *outrage*—which Sade understands to be the transgression of norms.

For Sade the fact of sensing, the irreducible element in perversion, does not have to be justified. It is the aberrant act issuing from sensuous nature that Sade wishes to moralize. This act is aberrant in the eyes of Sade himself, inasmuch as reason—even atheist reason—cannot recognize itself in it.

Sensuous nature is in Sade describable only in the form of a propensity to act. From this description Sade passes progressively to the moral explanation of the act. He thus establishes between the perverse way of sensing and the perverse way of acting the twofold relationship that the expression of one's own inwardness maintains with, on the one hand, the exteriority of an aberrant act and, on the other hand, the exteriority of normative reason. Then the distinction between deliberate sadism and an unreflecting sadistic act can be made only through the intervention of normative reason. The result is an indissoluble whole, in which the sensuous (that is, the experience peculiar to Sade) is obscured to the extent that discourse has to justify the act.

It is because of his way of conceiving of the act, which proceeds from the perverse way of sensing, that Sade declares himself to be an atheist. Conceiving the perverse act as obedience to a moral imperative, an idea, he constructs a new conception of perverse sensibility on the basis of this idea. He explicitly reorganizes the insubordination of the life functions on the basis of atheist reason and implicitly disorganizes normative reason on the basis of this functional insubordination.

Why Sade Did Not Seek a Positive Conceptual Formulation of Perversion (That Is, of Sensuous Polymorphy). The Necessity of Outrage

If Sade had sought (given that he would ever have been concerned with such a thing) a positive conceptual formulation of perversion, he would have passed by the enigma he sets up; he would not have intellectualized the phenomenon of sadism properly so-called. The motive for this is more obscure, and it forms the node of the Sadean experience: this motive is *outrage*. In outrage what is outraged is maintained to serve as a support for transgression.

Sade shuts himself up in the sphere of normative reason not only because he remains dependent on logically structured language but because the constraint exercised by the existing institutions comes to be individuated in the fatality of his own existence.

If one removes from consideration the intimate connivance between the expressive forces and those that are subversive—a connivance that was established in Sade's mind because he forces reason to serve as a reference for anomaly, and forces anomaly to refer to reason via the detour of atheism—then outrage will no longer be necessary in order that there be transgression. It becomes a purely intellectual transgression confounded with the general insurrection of minds on the eve of the Revolution. Sadism itself would then be but one utopian ideology among others.

But if, in Sade, outrage is necessary, then transgression must prevail over the postulates that derive logically from his atheist declarations.

The Theme of Transgression Makes Sade's Postulate of Integral Atheism Contradictory

Integral atheism means that the principle of identity itself disappears along with the absolute guarantor of this principle; the property of having a responsible ego is therewith morally and physically abolished. The first consequence will be the universal prostitution of beings. And this is but the counterpart of integral monstrosity, which rests on the insubordination of the life functions in the absence of any normative authority of the species.

Now the need for transgression paradoxically comes to oppose this twofold consequence of atheism. For the expropriation of the corporeal and moral self, the condition for universal prostitution, is still something that could be instituted, in the utopian sense of Fourier's phalanstery, which was based on the "interplay of the passions." As soon as this pooling together of the passions is established, there would no longer be the tension necessary for outrage, and sadism would dissipate—unless one knowingly created rules to be broken, this being the "game" (as is indeed done in the secret societies imagined by Sade).

Transgression presupposes the existing order, the apparent maintenance of norms under which energy accumulates thereby making transgression necessary. Thus universal prostitution has meaning only in terms of the moral possession of an individual body. Without this notion of ownership, prostitution would lose its attraction, and the outrage would come to nothing. Unless, that is, in the state of institutionalized prostitution the outrage would consist in inflicting the intrinsic ownership of a body on an individual who had been excluded from the universal pooling together.

Similarly for integral monstrosity as countergenerality implicit in the existing generality: perversion (the insubordination of the life functions), in the acts it inspires (particularly the sodomist act), derives its transgressive value only from the permanence of norms (such as the normative differentiation of the sexes). To the extent that perversion is more or less latent in individuals, it serves only as a model proposed to "normal" individuals as a way of transgression, just as the fact that one pervert may find a kindred spirit in another makes possible a mutual surpassing of their particular case.

If the human race as a whole "degenerated," if there were no one left but avowed perverts—if integral monstrosity would thus prevail—one might think that Sade's "goal" would have been reached, that there would no longer be any "monsters" and "sadism" would disappear. This perspective is precisely the snare of an "optimistic" interpretation of Sade, which, in its desire to credit the "psychopathological"—and therefore therapeutic—"value" in Sade's work, conjures away the enigma. But the ruse in the phenomenon that forms Sade's physiognomy lies in pretending to have a "goal," even a "scientific" one. This ruse resides in the underlying intuition that integral monstrosity can be realized only within the conditions that made sadism possible, within a space composed of obstacles, that is, in the logically structured language of norms and institutions. The absence of logical structure can be verified only through the given logic, even when it is the false logic that by refusing monstrosity provokes it. In turn monstrosity or anomaly, according to Sade, brings out the given norms and affirms itself only negatively. It is not surprising then that in Sade's descriptions the norms, the existing institutions, structure the very form of perversions. Nor is it surprising that Sade made no effort to formulate the positive content of perversion with new concepts. It is not the concept of nature in Sade—a concept originating in Spinoza and which Sade takes as "nature destructive of her own works"—that will explain the phenomenon of transgression. For, he says, nature destroys because "she seeks to recover her own most active power." This concept serves only as an argument for murder, for the insignificance of murder, as well as for refuting the law of the propagation of the species. It does not elucidate the transgressive pleasure, which aspires after *nothing*, save to renew itself.

Transgression (outrage) seems absurd and puerile when it does not succeed in resolving itself into a state of affairs in which it would no longer be necessary. But it belongs to the nature of transgression that it is never able to find such a state. Transgression is then something else than the pure explosion of an energy accumulated thanks to an obstacle. It is an incessant recuperation of the possible itself—inasmuch as the existing state of things has eliminated the possibility of another form of existence. The possible in what does not exist can never be anything but possible, for if the act were to recuperate this possible as a new form of existence, it would have to transgress it in turn. The possible as such would thus have been eliminated and would have to be recuperated yet again. What the act of transgression recuperates from the possible in what does not exist is *its own possibility of transgressing what exists.*

Transgression remains a necessity inherent in Sade's experience, independent of the interpretation he gives of it. It is not only because it is given out as a testimony of atheism that transgression must not and never can find a state in which it could be resolved; the energy must constantly be surpassed in order to verify its level. It falls below the level reached as soon as it no longer meets an obstacle. A transgression must engender another transgression. But if it is thus reiterated, in Sade it principally reiterates itself only through the *same act*. This very act can never be transgressed; its image is each time represented as though it had never been carried out.

Sade's Critique of the Pervert, the Preliminary for the Creation of a Sadean Character

To arrive at his notion of integral monstrosity, and to create an original character type to represent it, Sade first had to undertake a critique of the pervert properly so-called.

The pathological sense of the term *perversion* is not to be found in Sade. His terminology in this domain remains that of moral psychology, of the *examination of conscience* developed by the casuists.

In *The 120 Days of Sodom* the different cases of perversion are designated as passions, advancing from *simple passions* to *complex passions*. The whole set forms that genealogical tree of vices and crimes already evoked in *Aline and Valcour*. The subject affected with perversity is termed vicious, depraved, a "lecherous criminal," indulging in "murders in debauchery." The recurring term that is closest to notions of modern pathology is the term *maniac*.

Indeed the pervert Sade observes and describes in *The 120 Days*—that is, in the narration of anecdotes about and episodes in brothels, which will serve as themes that the four principal characters will be able to vary and improvise on—the pervert thus observed and documented does behave essentially as a maniac. He subordinates his pleasure to the performing of one sole gesture.

The pervert is distinguished in the midst of ordinary licentious company by a specific *fixed idea*. This is not yet the "idea" in the sense that Sade will work out. In the context of what one now calls "libertinage" nothing is less free than the pervert's gesture. For if one means by libertinage the pure and simple propensity for orgy, as free of scruples as can be, the pervert's desire is sated only in the scrupulous taste for, and search for, a detail, sated only in a gesture that advances scrupulously to this detail. This kind of concern escapes those who deliver themselves over to outbursts of raw appetites.

The pervert pursues the performance of one sole gesture; it is done in a moment. The pervert's existence becomes the constant waiting for the moment in which this gesture can be performed.

The pervert as such can signify himself only by this gesture; the executing of this gesture counts for the whole of his existing. As a result, the pervert has nothing to say about his gesture that would be intelligible on the level of reciprocity between individuals. The pervert is both below and beyond the level of "individuals," which level constitutes a set of functions subordinated to the norms of the species. He presents an arbitrary subordination of the habitual life functions to one sole insubordinate function, a craving for an improper object. In this respect he is not yet at the level of the most crude individuals. But inasmuch as this insubordination of one sole function could only be concretized and thus become individuated in his case, he suggests to Sade's reflections a multifold possibility of the redistribution of the functions. Beyond individuals "normally" constituted, he opens a broader perspective, that of sensuous polymorphy. In the conditions of life of the human species, the pervert is one who can affirm himself only by destroying these conditions in himself. His existence consecrates the death of the species in him as an individual; his being is verified as a suspension of life itself. Perversion would thus correspond to a property of being, a property founded on the expropriation of life functions. An expropriation of one's own body and of others would be the meaning of this property of being.

The pervert—whatever the sort of perversion that affects him—seems to formulate by his gesture a definition of existence and a sort of judgment put on existence. For his gesture to verify in this way the fact of existing, it must correspond to a representation. What the gesture designates is not comprehensible in itself. Though it is produced in a sphere of license, the pervert's gesture can be understood only as diverted from its incomprehensible content. In this sphere one discerns in this gesture only a detour to the sating of an appetite, which then apparently finds the same solution as "normal" appetites.

In Sade's eyes, the perverse gesture must have a signification that gets obscured in the closed circuit of a particular case of perversion. The perverse gesticulation is a deaf-mute language. Deaf-mutes possess a memory of their code, but the pervert's gesture does not yet belong to any code. His perversity is its own memory. It is not so much the pervert that recalls his gesture so as to unleash it again as it is the gesture itself that recalls the pervert.

If this gesture signifies something intelligible, if it answers to a representation, if finally it is a judgment, this means that this gesture *interprets* something. To make it explicit, Sade will interpret the supposed interpretation of the pervert. He will do so on the basis of what he deciphers in the pervert's gesture.

An absolutely central case of perversity, which Sade will take as the basis for interpreting all others, as the principle of affinity in what will form integral monstrosity, is the case of sodomy.

This biblical term, consecrated by moral theology, covers an action that is not limited to homosexual practice. Homosexuality, which is not an intrinsic perversion, must be distinguished from sodomy, which is. Like heterosexual forms of behavior, homosexual practices admit of giving rise to an institution, as has been seen many times in the history of human societies. But sodomy is formulated by a specific gesture of countergenerality, the most significant in Sade's eyes—that which strikes precisely at the law of the propagation of the species and thus *bears witness to the death of the species in the individual*. It evinces an attitude not only of refusal but of aggression; in being the simulacrum of the act of generation, it is a mockery of it. In this sense it is also a simulacrum of the destruction that a subject dreams of ravaging on another of the same sex by a sort of reciprocal transgression of their limits. When perpetrated on a subject of the other sex, it is a *simulacrum of metamorphosis*, always accompanied by a sort of magic fascination. The sodomist gesture, transgressing the organic specificity of individuals, introduces into existence the principle of the metamorphosis of beings into one another, which integral monstrosity tends to reproduce and which universal prostitution, the ultimate application of atheism, postulates.

To decipher the pervert's gesture Sade will set up a code of perversion. Its key sign is revealed by the constitution of the sodomist gesture. For Sade, all things, closeup or far-off, gravitate about this gesture—the more absolute because of the mortal threat it poses for the norms of the species, and also because of a kind of immortality its repetition gives it; the more ambiguous in that it is conceivable only because of the existence of these norms; the more qualified for transgression, which can be brought about only through the obstacle constituted by these norms.

One can see that Sade in no way seeks to know the origin of perversion with respect to norms, nor to explain how these norms could become depraved in the individual. He takes perversion as a given (constitutional or congenital) phenomenon that, like everything manifested by nature, is to be explained rationally. This is why Sade introduces logically structured language into perversion, which is with respect to this language a structure apparently devoid of logic.

The code, now translated into words, will feel the effects specifically of the perverse gesture on which it will be structured, as also logical language will restructure the perverse gesture and shape Sade's written expression of it. What logical language, as the language of reason, will adapt to the coded gesture of the pervert is atheism, as an "act of good sense," of "common sense." On the other hand, what the perverse gesture thus coded introduces into the language of "common sense" is the nonlanguage of monstrosity, which subsists under this code. Here, between the rational language of norms and the anomaly, there is a sort of osmosis that Sade alone could carry off—atheism will become integral only inasmuch as perversion will set out to be rational, and only inasmuch as it will have set out to be rational will it become integral monstrosity.

Here Sade will inaugurate his original creation by a decisive masterstroke: to create the imaginative character corresponding to the type of the pervert he conceives, Sade takes the pervert out of conventional licentious society, and in particular out of the brothel. Here Sade breaks with the libertine literary tradition and introduces the theme of perversion into the depiction of common manners of life. Sade plants his character in the everyday world; he finds him in the midst of institutions, in the fortuitous circumstances of social life. Thus the world itself appears as the locus in which the secret law of the universal prostitution of beings is verified. Sade conceives the countergenerality to be thus already implicit in the existent generality, not in order to criticize institutions, but in order to demonstrate that of themselves institutions ensure the triumph of perversions.

Sade invents a type of pervert who speaks with his singular gesture *in the name of generality*. If this gesture counts as a judgment, the judgment is pronounced only at the moment when the notion of generality intervenes. For if the gesture is singular, undecipherable, it is so only with respect to the generality of gestures. The generality of gestures is one with speech. It is true that if his gesture has a meaning for the pervert, he has no need of speech to express what it signifies by itself. But the singular gesture of the pervert is precisely not the gesture formed in the medium of generality that may accompany speech, is sometimes substituted for the word, and sometimes even contradicts it. The singular gesture of the pervert *empties all content out of speech at once, since it is by itself the whole of existence for him.*

But once set up as Sade's character type, the pervert explicates his singular gesture in accordance with the generality of gestures. By the very fact that he speaks, he requires the reciprocity involved in persuasion and invokes his belongingness to the human species.

It follows that the moment he speaks, the singularity of the gesture that was the motive of his discourse is disavowed in that such singularity is taken to be proper to each one. The content of his gesture is then not singular, for in silence it still had no meaning—and now it acquires meaning in speech. If, as the pervert says, the singularity of his gesture is proper to each, he still has to show that each one can act in the singular way that he acts. Yet each time the pervert speaks, it is only because he is convinced of the contrary—that he is alone in acting in this way. From the very fact that he speaks, he is mistaken about the object of his demonstration and raises up the obstacle established in himself. For the pervert who speaks, the obstacle is not to be singular but to belong to generality in his own singularity. How can he overcome this obstacle? If he speaks, can he show, in the name of generality, that there is no generality and that the norms of the species have no real existence? If that were true, one could no longer say that this singularity is proper to each. How could one show that the norms do not exist? The singularity of the gesture is reestablished without its opaqueness being in any way cleared up. The only one to have to show the validity of his gesture, the pervert makes haste to perform that gesture.

The discourse of the pervert, owing to the very fact that it invokes one's adherence to common sense, remains a sophism in that one does not get away from the concept of normative reason. Persuasion can be brought about only if the interlocutor is in turn led to reject norms in himself. It is not by arguments that Sade's character can obtain the assent of his interlocutor but by complicity.

Complicity is the contrary of persuasion in accordance with universal understanding. Those who know themselves to be accomplices in aberration need no argument to understand one another. Yet the characters Sade depicts, despite the affinities they discover in one another through the unique gesture (of sodomy), owe it to themselves to proclaim each time the absence of a God, guarantor of norms, and thus to profess the integral atheism that they claim to bear witness to by their acts. But among themselves, the coded gesture is disengaged from the logically structured language that, as an oratorical precaution, is put over it, and the key sign that this gesture represents reappears in its true locus: the secret society.

Here the gesture becomes a simulacrum, a rite, which the members of the secret society do not explain to one another otherwise than by the inexistence of the absolute guarantor of norms, an inexistence they commemorate as an event that one can represent only by this gesture.

In order for complicity with the pervert to emerge in the normal interlocutor, he qua "rational" individual must first be disintegrated. This is possible only by a leap of impulsion or of repulsion provoked in him by the word of the pervert.

How could the pervert recognize complicity in this "normal" interlocutor? By a gesture a subject makes in the generality of gestures, in contradiction to what he says. The interlocutor who rejects the sophism of the pervert makes a gesture that is in this sense contradictory, for, notwithstanding the disavowal it expresses, it physically, hence corporeally, bears witness to his own singularity—latent in him as in everyone. For if the rejection of the sophism is made in the name of the generality of common sense, what is the interlocutor, who at this moment has become a passive subject, defending himself against if not this latent singularity in himself? He can make this gesture of disavowal and defense only by thereby avowing his own singularity. The pervert lays in wait for this contradictory gesture, this reflex gesture, this corporeal, thus mute, gesture, which he deciphers in these terms: "Consider all the fatalities that unite us and see if Nature does not offer you a victim in my individual nature."

How Integral Monstrosity Constitutes a Space for Minds: The Ascesis of Apathy

For Sade, the sodomist act is the supreme form of the transgression of norms (which supposes their paradoxical maintenance); at the same time it must be the way to transgress the different cases of perversion and thus to constitute the principle of affinity among the perversions. For, like a callipygian test, this act suppresses the specific borders between the sexes and according to Sade constitutes the key sign for all perversions.

Having interpreted this act morally as a testimony of atheism and a declaration of war on the norms inherited from monotheism, Sade then projects perversion into the domain of thought. There integral monstrosity forms a sort of space for minds that communicate with one another by the mutual understanding of this key sign.

Whence the doctrinal character of Sade's work and of the didactic situations he lays out; whence above all the preliminary discrimination in effect in this singular academy by which the doctors of monstrosity recognize one another, distinguish themselves from the pervert shut up in his isolated case, and choose their disciples.

No candidate for integral monstrosity is recognized as qualified who has not conceived this way of acting as a profession of atheism; no atheist is recognized who is not capable of passing immediately into action. Once such disciples are chosen, they are subjected to a progressive initiation that culminates in the practice of an asceticism—the ascesis of apathy.

The practice of apathy, as Sade suggests it, supposes that what is named "soul," "consciousness," "sensibility," "the heart," are only diverse structures that the concentration of the same impulsive forces take on. These forces can set up the structure of an instrument of intimidation under the pressure of the institutional world or that of an instrument of subversion under the internal pressure of these forces, and they set up these structures in an instantaneous movement. But it is always the same impulses that intimidate us at the same time that they raise us up in revolt.

How does this intimidating insurrection or this insurrectional intimidation act in us? By the images that precede the acts, inciting us to act or to undergo, as well as by the images of acts committed or omitted that recur in us and make our conscience remorseful whenever the idleness of the impulses reconstitutes it. Thus the consciousness of oneself and of others is a most fragile and most transparent structure.

Since our impulses intimidate us in the form of "fear," "compassion," "horror," "remorse," by images of acts that have been or can be realized, it is the acts, whatever they be, that we must substitute for their repellent images whenever these images tend to substitute themselves for the acts and thus to forestall them.

Sade does not use the term *image* here; it is we who put this term in place of the terms *fear* and *remorse,* since his terms presuppose a representation of the act that has been or has to be committed. Yet an image intervenes not only in the form of remorse but also in the form of a project.

Reiteration is at first the condition required for the monster to remain on the level of monstrosity; if the reiteration is purely passionate it remains uncertain. For the monster to progress beyond the level that has been reached, he has first to avoid falling back shy of it; he can do so only if he reiterates his act in absolute apathy. This alone can maintain him in a state of permanent transgression. In putting this new condition on the candidate for integral monstrosity, Sade introduces a critique of the sensuous, and especially a critique of the primary benefit of transgression—the pleasure inseparable from the act.

How can the same act committed in intoxication, in delirium, be reiterated sobermindedly? For there to be any possibility of reeffecting this act, must not the image which re-presents itself to the mind, however repellent it be, function as a lure, a promise of pleasure?

What Sade takes as understood beneath his maxim of the apathetic reiteration of an act we can reconstitute as follows: Sade recognizes the alternation of the diverse structures that the impulsive forces take on in their insurrectional and at the same time intimidating movement. But in one of these structures that these forces, individuated in the subject, have developed under the pressure of the institutional environment, that is, of norms, he seems also to have recognized a *self-consciousness*. This structure suffers variations and instability, though these become clear only after the event. Sometimes these forces put the subject *outside of himself* and make him act *against himself;* they transgress the structure of consciousness and decompose it. Sometimes, in particular when they have made him act against himself, they recompose the (remembering) consciousness of the subject during his inaction; in this case these same forces are inverted. The inversion of the same forces constitutes the consciousness that *censors* the subject. What exercises censorship is the feeling the subject has that *being put outside of oneself* is a menace to the subject, who is dependent on the norms of the species. This censorship is exercised already in the very act of transgression and is the necessary motive for it. For Sade, moral conscience simply corresponds to an exhaustion of the impulsive forces (the "calm of the senses"); this state of exhaustion opens an interval in which the repellent image of the act committed represents itself in the form of "remorse."

In fact, from the first time the act was committed, it presented itself as a promise of pleasure because its image was repellent. And if now the reiteration of the same act is to "annihilate" conscience, it is because each time it is the same forces that, through their inversion, reestablish conscience. Inverted into a censorship, they will then provoke the act again.

Sade's formulation of apathetic reiteration is the expression of a deeper apprehension: Sade feels quite clearly that transgression is bound up with censorship, but the purely logical analysis that his formulation presupposes does not grasp the contradictory simultaneity of the two. Sade describes and decomposes this simultaneity into successive states: insurrection-transgression-intimidation; but intimidation and transgression remain in close interdependency, each provoking the other. This is why he wishes to eliminate intimidation by the apathetic reiteration of the act. He then apparently empties transgression of the benefit it would yield: pleasure.

The elimination of the sensuous element should then block the return of moral conscience. But in preventing its return, this ascesis seems to uproot the motive for transgression. The sodomist act (which forms the key sign of all perversion) has no significative value save as a conscious transgression of the norms represented by conscience. The being cast *outside of oneself* thus sought for is in practice equivalent to a disintegration of the conscience of the subject by means of thought. Thought must reestablish the primitive version of the impulsive forces, which the conscience of the subject has inverted. For the disciple who will practice the doctrine (not the pervert shut up in his own singular case), monstrosity is the zone of this being *outside of oneself, outside of conscience;* the monster can maintain himself in this zone only by the reiteration of the same act. The "voluptuous harshness" that, according to Sade, is its fruit is no longer something sensuous: the "harshness" presupposes a distinction between thought and moral conscience; the "voluptuousness" alludes to the ecstasy of thought in the representation of the act reiterated "in cold blood"—an ecstasy here opposed to its functional analogue, orgasm.

For the orgasmic moment amounts to a fall of thought outside of its own ecstasy. It is this fall outside of ecstasy that ends in the orgasm of the body's functions that Sade's character wishes to prevent through apathy. He knows that orgasm is but a tribute paid to the norms of the species and is thus a counterfeit of the ecstasy of thought. It is not enough that orgasm in the sodomist act is but a loss of forces, a *useless* pleasure; when the act, this time separated from orgasm, is reiterated, this useless pleasure is identified with the ecstasy of thought.

The apathetic reiteration of the act brings to light a new factor—number—and in particular the relationship between quantity and quality in sadism. The act passionately reiterated on the same object depreciates (or varies) in favor of the quality of the object. As the object is multiplied and as the number of objects depreciates them, so the quality of the act itself, reiterated in apathy, is the better affirmed.

The Lesson of Apathy: Is
Transgression of the Act Possible?

It could be that for thought apathetic reiteration is but a parable and that transgression ends by transgressing the act: "Virtue itself will safeguard you from remorse, for you shall have acquired the habit of doing evil at the first virtuous prompting; and to cease doing evil you shall have to stifle virtue."[3]

Let us see if this second maxim contradicts or corroborates the maxim of apathetic reiteration. We take note that it says, "You shall have acquired the habit of doing evil . . . and to cease doing evil." There are here two ways of acting such that the first substitutes itself for the second and makes nonrepentance into virtue, which will now consist in "ceasing to do evil."

The coordinate clause introduced by "for" (*qua re*) incriminates as the motive for repentance "the habit of doing evil at the first virtuous prompting." Hence there is a connection between two kinds of reaction: repentance, which is but a reaction undergone by the subject; and the habit of doing evil upon sight of virtue, a habit which is a reflex, that of reacting immediately with an outrage. A first conclusion to be drawn is that repentance and the habit of doing evil are equally negative reflexes. If that is the case, the second maxim (stifle virtue) aims to substitute for the reflex of outrage a reaction to this reflex (a reaction against the necessity of outrage), which would then be a positive action.

"You shall have acquired the habit of doing evil . . . "—is this not the purpose of the deliberate apathetic reiteration? Then when will this reiteration no longer be a habit of doing evil? If it is a transposition, a *deliberate* reflex, how can it be distinguished from the habit of doing evil, the habit of perpetrating an outrage? If the deliberate reflex cannot be distinguished from the habit, then the second injunction would appear to be in fact the refutation of the apathetic reiteration. For the second phrase to be, to the contrary, the explanation of that reiteration, one has to see how it disengages from the simple reacting characteristic of outrage a positive acting without outrage, by preventing virtue from showing itself. How does virtue show itself—in what intolerable aspect? It shows itself as consistency (that of the conscious subject); consistency represents the Good. According to the principle of identity that follows from individuation, inconsistency is Evil. But for the impulsive forces that bear ill will against individuation, inconsistency is Good. Since the impulsive forces maintain inconsistency but manifest themselves only in terms of consistency, which is intolerable to them, they must then themselves acquire *constancy* in inconsistency. In other words, Sade wished to transgress the act of outrage by a permanent state of perpetual movement—that movement which Nietzsche much later named "the innocence of becoming." But Sade caught sight of this transgression of transgression by itself only for a moment; the hyperbole of his thought brings him back to the core of his irreducible sensibility bound to its representation of an outrageous act—which excludes the very notion of innocence. That is why the impulsive forces can prevent virtue, that is, consistency, from showing itself only through the constancy of an act, its reiteration, which, however apathetic it is, is but a reiterated reconstitution of the intolerable aspect of virtue as well as of the outrage this aspect provokes.

Androgyny in Sade's Representation

In Sade the principal types of perversion are generally represented only by men; the number of unnatural women found there do not really represent anomaly as such. Man, because traditionally he alone exercises reflection, represents the rational sex; he is also therefore alone called upon to give an account of reason. However monstrous, perverse, delirious a woman may be, she is never considered "abnormal," for it is written in the norms that by nature she lacks reflection, possesses no equilibrium or measure, and never represents anything but uncontrolled sensuous nature, more or less attenuated by a reflection prescribed by man. Indeed, the more monstrous or mad she is the more fully a woman she is, according to the traditional representation, always colored by misogyny. Yet she has resources that man will never possess, resources she shares with the pervert.

The integral monstrosity conceived by Sade has as its immediate effect the working of an exchange of the specific qualities of the sexes. The result is not just a simple symmetrical reversal of the schema of differentiation within each of the two sexes, with active and passive pederasty on the one side, lesbianism and tribadism on the other. In integral monstrosity as a didactic project for sensuous polymorphousness, the two representatives of the species, male and female, will in their relationship with one another face a twofold model. Each of the two sexes interiorizes this twofold model not only because of the ambivalence proper to each but also because of the embellishment Sade put on this ambivalence.

Man as the Sadean pervert type, although he apparently retains rational primacy, henceforth presents himself as the assertion of sensuous nature, but in the sense that sensuous nature offers itself to him in the perspective of the mind: the perspective of the imaginary. Perversion, we said at the beginning, insofar as it confirms the fact of its being by a suspension of the life functions, would correspond to a property of being whose meaning would be the expropriation of one's own body and the body of the other.

Integral atheism, the suppression of an absolute guarantor of norms, would corroborate this expropriation ideologically. For in abolishing the limits of the responsible and self-identical ego, it logically abolishes the identity of one's own body. In itself the body is the concrete product of the individuation of the impulsive forces realized according to the norms of the species. Since we are in fact dealing with denomination in language, we can say now that these impulsive forces speak to the pervert in these terms: The language of institutions has taken over this body, more particularly taken over what is functional in *"my"* body for the best preservation of the species. This language has assimilated the body that "I am" through this body to the point that "we" have been expropriated by institutions from the beginning. This body has only been restored to "me" corrected in certain ways—certain forces have been pruned away, others subjugated by language. "I" then do not possess "my" body save in the name of institutions; the language in "me" is just their overseer put in "me." Institutional language has taught "me" that this body in which "I am" was "mine." The greatest crime "I" can commit is not so much to take "his" body from the "other"; it is to break "my" body away from this "myself" instituted by language. What "I" gain by "myself" having a body, "I" immediately lose in reciprocal relations with the "other," whose body does not belong to "me."

The representation of having a body whose state is not that of one's own body is clearly specific to perversion. Although the pervert feels the alterity of the alien body, he feels much more the body of the other as being his own, and the body that normatively and institutionally is his he experiences as being really foreign to himself, that is, foreign to the insubordinate function that defines him. For him to be able to conceive the effect of his violence on the other, he must first inhabit the other. In the reflexes of another's body he verifies this foreignness; he experiences the irruption of an alien force within "himself." He is both within and without.

How can this be brought about? Not first, indeed not at all by recourse to violence that could go as far as murder, but rather by the imagination that precedes every violent act. The imaginary will have primacy over the rational. We can see this primacy of the imaginary in the representation of pleasure, where the impulse doubles up in the projecting of an image of itself, extending pleas-

ure to organs excluded from the function of propagation and reducing the functional organs, thereby producing pleasure without
utility.

The imagination prerequisite for the perverse gesture is constituted on correspondences between intensities that the functional reason had to exclude in order to set itself up on the basis of
the subordination of the life functions of the species. While reason
(logical language) expresses and also guarantees the equilibrium
that the species found in its empirical habit, imagination appre-
hends the schemas of an illusory function in which the existing
organ only serves to take the place of the absent—hence ideal—
"functional" structure. In these schemas, the absence of the structure that is imagined is evidently the factor that excites; the existing
structures offer a terrain in which outrage is inflicted in the name
of something absent: the ideal structure of the androgynous one.

When the presence of this imaginary structure in the pervert
and his disconnection from his body are strong enough for him to
behave as a woman with his masculine counterpart, he will feel feminine passivity in himself more profoundly. He can then conduct
himself *actively* only if he deals with his masculine counterpart as
with a woman, or deals with a woman as with a boy.

Out of this latter case, Sade elaborates the synthetic simulacrum of the androgynous being—not a woman-man but a man-
woman. He conceived Juliette as such a being. Contrary to man,
more particularly contrary to the Sadean pervert, who, in integral
monstrosity, functions as the definition of sensuous nature, the
Sadean heroine sets forth reason. She makes use of reason only the
better to recover possession of sensuous nature, which she originally
and traditionally (according to the norms) is; she recovers possession
of that sensuous nature only inasmuch as she progresses into insen-
sibility. She presents the perfect example of the morality of apathy.
This morality is one of the secret expedients of women, here set up
as a doctrine; the morality of apathy is feminine frigidity methodically put to use. Finally, and most important, it is the Sadean heroine

who carries atheism all the way to its integral affirmation, dissociating it from normative and anthropomorphic reason, freeing thought itself in the experimental sphere of monstrosity.

The abolition of norms, which this thought implies, is more important to the woman than to the pervert, in whom the norms exist only in a state of decay. As woman she remains subject to the norms at least organically, principally by reason of her fecundable condition. All the more then will she seek in apathy her line of conduct, the first effect of which is the extirpation of all maternal instinct. Here again we see verified the fact that the norms themselves (here corporeal norms) as institutions structure the forces that are to destroy them. "Normally" prostitutable, "normally" vicious, "normally" lesbian and tribade, it is again reason, here "good sense," that dictates to her that she be all this coldly. In learning to undergo coolly the perverse acts committed on her own body, she develops the virile energy of a consummate callipygian.

Thus Juliette presents herself to the Sadean pervert as the simulacrum of what the sodomist act designates. In this figure formed by the reversal of sensuous passivity into active intellection, the preeminent act of transgression finds the image complementary to it.

How the Sadist Experience Renders Unreadable the Conventional Form of Communication

In what has preceded I have sought to examine the *interpretive* character of the description Sade gives of his own experience. This experience appeared to include a twofold experimentation: that of the representation of sensuous nature in an aberrant act, and that of its described representation. We must return to the fact that Sade writes a work. What is the literary character of this work? How does its singularity set it apart not only from its contemporary literary context but from everything one defines as literature? Is it essentially modern, or does it elude this definition also? Let us look more closely into the question formulated earlier: How does sensuous nature get actualized in an aberrant act by writing, and what is the relationship between this actualization and the perpetration of the act independent of its description?

Dealing with a personal experience condemned by its very nature to remain incommunicable, Sade chooses to translate this experience into the conventional form characteristic of all communication. Then the conventional communication becomes "unreadable" each time the incommunicable experience asserts itself, but becomes all the more readable when this experience disappears again. How does Sade's experience render his conventional form of communication "unreadable"? In that it is built entirely on reiteration. The object of reiteration is to arouse an ecstasy. This ecstasy cannot be conveyed by language; what language describes are the ways to it, the dispositions that prepare for it. But what does not get brought out clearly in Sade's conventional form of writing is that the ecstasy and the reiteration are the same thing. In the description the fact of reiterating and that of undergoing the ecstasy are two different aspects. For the reader there remains only the reiteration described and the wholly exterior aspect of the ecstasy, the orgasm described, which is counterfeit ecstasy.

Sade seems to represent his reader as someone he must continually keep gasping with the promise of yet another shock. Yet what the reader is seeking in the end at the expense of his reading is a sort of lapse of attention at a moment when the whole text wants sustained attention, a lapse of the thought pursued so laboriously. Here what is required is that we compare the practice of writing with the principle of the apathetic reiteration of acts. This principle has an immediate effect on Sade's literary expression; it is at work in what that literary expression contains that is apparently nonliterary, unreadable in the broad sense of the term. The apathetic reiteration conveys Sade's own struggle to regain possession of what is irreducible in his experience. It defines the bottom layer of this experience; the actualization of the aberrant act by writing corresponds to the apathetic reiteration of this act itself perpetrated independently of its description. In actualizing the act, writing works up the ecstasy of thought; reiterated on the level of language, this ecstasy coincides with the transgression reiterated by fictitious characters. Thus the logically structured language with which Sade expresses himself becomes for him the terrain of outrage, as it is the terrain of norms.

If Sade expresses himself in logically structured language, it is because this language has also structured in advance the depth of Sade's own experience. In order to make that experience clear to himself through his writing, he could apprehend it only in accordance with the laws of this language—by transgressing them. He never transgresses these laws except in the gesture whereby he reproduces them *in* their transgression. Is it then the logical structure of language—or is it the very core of the experience—that wills the reiteration of outrage? No doubt it is this core of experience, already structured by language, but restructuring its logic on the basis of the aberrant act.

Traditional language, which Sade himself uses with amazing effect, can put up with everything that conforms with its logical structure. It corrects, censors, excludes, or silences everything that would destroy this structure—all non-sense. To *describe* aberration is to set forth positively the absence of elements that make a thing, a state, a being not viable. This logical structure Sade accepts and maintains without discussion; what is more, he develops it, systematizes it, even in outraging it. For he outrages it by conserving it only as a dimension of aberration—not because aberration is described in this logically structured language, but because the aberrant act is *reproduced* in it.

To reproduce the aberrant act in this way amounts to giving language as a possibility of the action; whence the irruption of nonlanguage in language.

When Suetonius describes Caligula's or Nero's aberrant acts, it is not to maintain beyond these men the possibility of these acts *in his text*. Nor is it to identify his text with the maintenance of this possibility.

Sade's text maintains and supports the possibility of the aberrant act, inasmuch as the writing actualizes this act. Yet this actualization by writing acts as a censorship that Sade inflicts on himself, a censorship put on an act that could be perpetrated independently of its description. The image of the aberrant act has first become a logically structured aberration. Thus structured in discourse, the aberration exhausts reflection; the words become again what the discourse had for a moment prevented them from being—a propensity for the very act that reestablishes the image of its perpetration in muteness. Why in muteness? Because the motive of the act to be done, the outrage, is not recognized in the sort of monumentalization of the possibility for action that speech, words, the phrasing of discourse produce. The discourse buried the act that was to be committed, even as it exalted its image. The propensity for the aberrant act then destroys this funerary image and once again requires obedience to its motive. Thus it precipitates anew the description of the act that here *stands for* its perpetration but can do so only as *recommenced.*

The parallelism between the apathetic reiteration of acts and Sade's descriptive reiteration again establishes that the image of the act to be done is re-presented each time not only as though it had never been performed but also as though it had never been described. This reversibility of the same process inscribes the presence of *nonlanguage* in language; it inscribes a foreclosure of language by language.

"Foreclosure" means that something remains outside. That which remains outside is, once again, the act to be done. The less it is perpetrated the more it raps on the door—the door of literary vacuity. The blows struck on the door are Sade's words, which, if they now reverberate within literature, remain nonetheless blows

struck from without. The outside is what of itself dispenses with any
commentary. What gives Sade's text its disturbing originality is that
through him this outside comes to be commented on as something
produced within thought.

Do we read Sade as we read Laclos, Stendhal, Balzac? Clearly
not! We would not look to the bottom of the pages of *Splendors and
Miseries of the Courtesans* for notes that would give prescriptive for-
mulas and recipes for procedures to follow or ways to act in the
bedchamber. We do find here and there this sort of quite pragmatic note at the bottom of the pages of *Juliette*. Perhaps some of
these notes have been added for commercial reasons; perhaps they
are not even from Sade's hand. Yet they figure in the editions published during his lifetime. It would be false discretion to wish to
drop them from the text; they belong with the subject matter of the
book. To say that they are devoid of literary interest would be to
show one understands nothing of Sade's originality. These pragmatic notes belong to the exercise of his purest irony. The irony
would have no object if these notes were without real pragmatic
use. In any case, they function to indicate the outside. This outside
is not at all the interior of the "bedroom" where one would philos-
ophize; it is the inwardness of thought which *nothing* separates
from the "bedroom."

In fact the term *bedroom* is a riddle; in Sade it designates the
bloody cave of the Cyclops, whose one eye is that of voracious
thought.

Thus the foreclosure of language by itself gives Sade's work its
singular configuration—first a set of tales, discourses, then a series
of tableaux that slyly invite the reader to see outside what does not
seem to lie in the text—whereas nothing is visible anywhere except
in the text. His work then is like the vast layout of an urban show-
room at the heart of a city, one with the city, where without noticing
it one passes from the objects exhibited to objects that exhibit themselves fortuitously without being exhibitable. At length one recognizes that it is to these that the corridors of the exhibition lead.

SADE MY
NEIGHBOR

Sade
and the
Revolution

1

Apparently the Revolution could break out only because of a vast combination of contradictory demands. If the existing psychic forces had identified one another at the start, their unanimous mobilization would never have come about. It was because of a kind of confusion between two different categories of demands that the subversive atmosphere could take form. There were, in fact, two groups in collusion. There was, on the one hand, the amorphous mass of average men who demanded a social order in which the idea of *natural man* could prove itself. "Natural man" was here but the idealization of the ordinary man, an ideal that especially attracted that portion of the people who had hitherto lived below the level of the ordinary man. But there was also a category of men belonging to the ruling classes and existing at a higher level of life, who, because of the iniquity of this level, were able to develop a supreme degree of lucidity. These men, grand bourgeois or enlightened aristocrats, dreamers or systematic minds, libertines in their minds or in practice, were able to objectify the content of their bad conscience; they knew the morally uncertain content of their existence, as they knew the problematic structure they had developed within themselves. If those of the one group desired to regenerate themselves in the course of the social upheaval and find their own solutions in that upheaval (this was the case with Chamfort), others, to the contrary, thought above all of having their own problematic structure admitted as a universal necessity; they awaited the Revolution as something that would bring about a complete remolding of the structure of man. This at any rate is the case for Sade; he is haunted by the image of integral man, a man of polymorphic sensibility.

There is in the course of the Revolution a period of collective incubation during which the first transgressions the masses commit can make one think that the people have become open to all kinds of adventures. This period of psychic regression, which turns out to be quite temporary, plunges libertine minds into a sort of euphoria: there is some chance that the most daring elaborations of individual thought will be put into practice. It now appears to them that what has ripened in their minds because of the degree of decomposition they have individually reached they will be able to sow on fertile ground. They cannot recognize that they are instead as it were the already rotten fruit that is detaching itself from the tree of society; they will fall because they are an end, not a beginning, the end of a long evolution. They forget that the ground receives only the seed, that is, only that part of the universal lesson that their example can hold for posterity. Their dream of giving birth to a humanity like themselves is in contradiction with the very basis of their ripeness, or their lucidity. It is only in the course of crises such as those they have passed through that other individuals, like themselves waste products of the collective process, will be able to reach the same degree of lucidity and thenceforth establish a genuine filiation with them.[1]

As now brutal and unforeseeable decisions of the masses intervene, as the hypostases of new factions are embodied and become laws while the moral and religious authorities of the old hierarchy are emptied of their content, these problematic men suddenly find themselves out of their element and disoriented. In fact they were closely bound up with the sacred values they spat upon. Their libertinage had meaning only at the level they occupied in the fallen society. Now that the throne has been overturned, the severed head of the king is trampled in the dust, the churches are sacked and sacrilege has become an everyday occupation of the masses, these immoralists come to look like eccentrics. They appear as they really were: symptoms of dissolution who have paradoxically survived the dissolution and who cannot integrate themselves into the process of recomposition which the hypostases of a sovereign people, a general will, etc., are bringing about in men's minds. It would be enough that these men go before the people and before them construct a system out of the fundamental necessity of sacrilege, massacre, and rape, for the masses, who have just committed these offenses, to turn against these philosophers and tear them to pieces with as much satisfaction.

It seems at first sight that there is here an insoluble problem: the man of privilege who has reached the supreme degree of consciousness because of a social upheaval is totally unable to make social forces benefit from his lucidity. He is incapable of making the individuals of the mass, which is amorphous but rich in possibilities, identical with himself even for a moment. He seems to occupy his morally advanced position to the detriment of the revolutionary mass. From the point of view of its own preservation, the mass is right, for each time the human mind takes on the incisive aspect of a physiognomy such as Sade's, it runs the risk of precipitating the end of the whole human condition. Yet the mass is wrong, since it is composed only of individuals, and the individual represents the species intrinsically; and there is no reason why the species should escape the risks involved for it in the success of an individual.

The more an individual is a success, the more he concentrates the diffuse energies of his age, the more dangerous he is for his age. But the more he concentrates in himself those diffuse energies to bring them to bear on his own destiny, the more he liberates the epoch from those energies. Sade made of the virtual criminality of his contemporaries his own personal destiny; he wished to expiate by himself that destiny in proportion to the collective guilt his consciousness had invested.

Saint-Just and Bonaparte, on the contrary, had known how to discharge on their fellows all that the age had accumulated in them. From the point of view of the masses they were perfectly sane men, and they themselves knew that the best index of the health of a man to whom the masses submit is his resolve to sacrifice them. From the point of view of the masses Sade is clearly an unhealthy man. Far from finding some kind of moral satisfaction in revolutionary violence, he was not far from experiencing the legalized carnage of the Terror as a caricature of his own system. During his imprisonment at Picpus, under Robespierre, he described his stay in these terms: "An earthly paradise—beautiful house, splendid garden, select society, admirable women—and then suddenly the place of the executions is put right under our windows and the cemetery of the guillotined right in the middle of our garden. We have, my dear friend, removed eighteen hundred guillotined in five days, including a third of our unhappy household" (29 Brumaire, year III).

Later, he wrote: "Amid everything I am not well; my state detention, with the guillotine right under my eyes, made me suffer a hundred times more than all the imaginable Bastilles ever had" (2 Pluviôse, year III). He then feels the need always to go further in his writings. It was not only because he at last had the right to say everything, but in order to somehow have a clear conscience for having given the lie to the truths proclaimed by the Revolution that he then put out the most virulent version of his *Justine.* Somewhere the secret impulse of the revolutionary mass had to be laid bare. For this impulse had not been laid bare in its political manifestations, since even when the revolutionary mass beat to death, drowned, hanged, pilloried, burned, and raped, it always did so in the name of the sovereign people.

SADE AND THE REVOLUTION

Sade's lifelong perseverance in studying only the perverse forms of human nature will prove that one thing alone mattered to him: the need to render to man all the evil he is capable of rendering. The republican state claims it exists for the public good; but if it is clear that the state cannot bring about the reign of the good, no one suspects that in its depths it nurtures the germs of evil. Under the pretense of preventing the germs of evil from hatching, the new social order claims itself victorious over evil. A constant threat lies in the depths of this order: the evil that never breaks out but can do so at any moment. This chance for evil to break out is the object of Sade's constant anxiety; evil has to break out once and for all, the tares have to flourish so that the spirit can tear them up and destroy them. It is necessary to make evil reign once and for all in the world in order that it destroy itself, and Sade's mind find peace at last. But there is no question of thinking of this peace; it is impossible to think of it for a moment because each moment is filled with the threat of evil, while freedom refuses to recognize that it lives only through evil and claims to exist for the sake of good.

Sade must necessarily experience the Jacobin Revolution as a detestable competitor that deforms his ideas and compromises his enterprise. Whereas Sade wanted to establish the kingdom of integral man, the Revolution wishes to make the natural man live. For this natural man, the Revolution enlists all the forces that in reality belong to integral man and should contribute to his expansion. There is no worse enemy of integral man than God, and in killing the king, the temporal representative of God, God was also killed in consciousness. This incommensurable murder could have only an incommensurable consequence: the coming of integral man. Integral man thus bears the seal of crime, of the most redoubtable of all crimes: regicide. "A most unusual thought comes to mind at this point, but if it is audacious it is also true, and I will mention it," Sade writes. "A nation that begins by governing itself as a republic will only be sustained by virtues because, in order to attain the most, one must always start with the least. But an already old and decayed nation which courageously casts off the yoke of its monarchical government in order to adopt a republican one will only be maintained by many crimes; for it is criminal already, and if it were to wish to pass from crime to virtue, that is to say, from a violent to a pacific, benign condition, it should fall into an inertia whose result would soon be its certain ruin."[2]

For Sade, the revolution that an old and decayed nation goes through could then in no way be an opportunity for regeneration. Once the nation has been purged of its aristocratic class there can be no question of inaugurating the blessed age of recovered natural innocence. For Sade, the regime of freedom should be, and in fact will be, nothing more or less than monarchical corruption taken to its limit. "An already old and decayed nation," that is, already arrived at a certain level of criminality, "will courageously cast off the yoke of monarchical government," that is, the level of criminality to which its old masters had brought it will make it able to commit regicide in order to adopt a republican government— that is, a social state that the perpetration of regicide will have brought to a greater level of criminality. The revolutionary community will then be at bottom secretly but inwardly bound up with the moral dissolution of monarchical society, since it is through this dissolution that the members have acquired the force and energy necessary for bloody decisions. And what else does corruption mean here if not the advanced state of dechristianization of society of which Sade is the contemporary—the practice of arbitrariness the more unrestrainable in that it had its foundations, if not in atheism, at least in the most profound skepticism?

In the measure that this moral skepticism, this instigating or convinced atheism, spread into monarchical society, monarchical society reached a state of decomposition such that the feudal relations between lord and servant consecrated by the theocratic hierarchy were already virtually broken: the ancient relationship of master and slave was de facto reestablished.

2. The Decomposition of the Theocratic
    Feudal Order and the Birth of
    Aristocratic Individualism

Between the ancient conditions of slavery and the Revolution, the
theocratic hierarchy was established in the West, an attempt by the
Church to group together existing social forces into an order that
could ensure for each category of individuals its own moral signification. The theocratic hierarchy was reputed to have put an end to the
ancient law of the jungle; man created in the image of God cannot
exploit man, every man is a servant of God. On the pediment of the
theocratic hierarchy is written the proverb: The fear of the Lord is
the beginning of wisdom. The king, appointed by God, is his temporal servant; the lord, appointed by the king, is the servant of the king;
and every man who recognizes that he is the servant of his lord is a
servant of God. The hierarchy assigns to the lord the military, juridical, and social functions with which he is invested by the king, and
which constitute for him obligations to the king and to the people;
but the exercise of these functions ensures him the right to recogni-
tion and to the fidelity of his vassal and servant. On his side, the
servant, put under the protection of his lord to whom he renders
homage and fidelity, makes an act of faith in his God and in his king.
Thus, at the lowest rung of the hierarchy, he finds his individual
significance because he participates in an edifice whose keystone is
God. In time the king concentrates more and more power in himself, while the lord abandons his functions one after another; the
lord progressively emancipates himself from his obligations to the
king but still claims to retain the privileges and rights that derive
from them. It is enough, then, for the lord to develop an existence
for himself and give his privileges the form of an enjoyment for
which he has no accounts to render to God or to anyone—to his
servant less than anyone else—it is enough that the lord put in
doubt the existence of God, and the whole edifice totters. In the eyes
of the servant, serving on the bottom of the social ladder loses all

meaning. Finally, when the lord seems to wish to maintain the edifice of the theocratic hierarchy for the sole purpose of his gratuitous existence, an existence that is the very negation of this hierarchy, an existence that consists in demonstrating that the fear of the Lord is the beginning of folly, then the law of the jungle returns in force. The conditions for the ancient relationships between strong and weak, master and slave, are back in place.

The libertine great lord, in particular, is on the eve of the Revolution a master who knows he is the legal wielder of power but who also knows that he can lose it at any moment and that he is already virtually a slave. Since in his own eyes he no longer has an uncontested authority, but still has the instincts of such authority, and since his will no longer has anything sacred about it, he adopts the language of the crowd and says he is a rake. He looks for arguments in the works of philosophers; he reads Hobbes, d'Holbach, and La Mettrie; no longer believing in divine right he seeks to legitimate his privileged state by the sophisms of reason available to anyone. In his privileged state, the libertine great lord, if he is not resolutely an atheist, conceives of his existence as a provocation addressed to God at the same time as to the people. If he is resolutely an atheist, in disposing of the life of his servant as he pleases, in making of him a slave, the object of his pleasure, he makes the people understand that he has killed God in his own mind and that his prerogatives were nothing but the practice of crime with impunity. But the man who on the lowest level of the hierarchy had joined with God in serving has, now that God is dead at the summit of the hierarchy, fallen into the condition of a slave. He still remains a servant, a servant without a lord, as long as God lives in his mind. He effectively becomes a slave only when, experiencing the death of God in his own consciousness, he continues to be subject to the one who is in fact the master. This man on the lowest level becomes virtually a master only insofar as, having assented to the murder of God perpetrated at the summit of the hierarchy, he will wish to annihilate the master to become master himself.

The servant who has become a slave as a result of atheism, or of the sacrilegious existence of his master, does indeed revolt; he then accepts the death of God. But when he goes to bring his master to trial, in the name of what will he do so, if not in the name of the prerogative of crime? He can only immediately become an accomplice in the revolt of his master against God and take up crime in his turn. The trial can have no other outcome but the assumption by the slaves of the prerogatives of the masters, and this will begin with the killing of the masters. Such, it seems, is indeed the vicious circle of the insidious thesis that claims that a nation that has cast off the yoke of its monarchic government will only be maintained by many crimes because it is already in crime—the vicious circle in which Sade wishes to enclose the Revolution.

The Republic, in short, can never begin; the Revolution is truly the Revolution only inasmuch as it is the monarchy in perpetual insurrection. A sacred value can be trampled underfoot only when one has it under one's feet. The theocratic principle is not in question; to the contrary, it determines Sade's terminology. For otherwise what would the word *crime* mean?

3. Regicide, the Simulacrum of the Putting to Death of God

The putting to death of the king by the nation is then only the final phase of the process whose first phase is the putting to death of God by the revolt of the libertine great lord. The execution of the king thus becomes the simulacrum of the putting to death of God. When, after having judged the king, whose person was until the suspension of the monarchy inviolable, the men of the Convention are called upon to pronounce for or against condemnation to death, the thesis that will draw most of the votes in favor of capital punishment will be, could only be, a compromise between the juridical and the political points of view. Only some isolated participants, taking up the act of defiance being made against monarchist Europe, will dare say with Danton: We do not wish to condemn the king, we wish to kill him. Even Saint-Just, preoccupied above all with inculcating in the nation a firm sentiment of its rights, affirms that it is less a matter of judging the king than of combating him as an enemy—because one cannot reign innocently. But it will be Robespierre, conscious of the necessity of creating a new notion of public law, who will put the dilemma in decisive terms: "There is here no trial to be conducted. Louis is not a culprit; you are not judges. You are, you could only be, statesmen, representatives of the nation. You do not have a sentence to pronounce for or against a man; you have a measure of public health to take, an action of national providence to exercise. For if Louis can still be the object of a trial, he can be absolved, he can be innocent—what am I saying, he is presumed to be innocent until he is judged. But if Louis is absolved, if Louis can be presumed innocent, what becomes of the revolution? If Louis is innocent, all the defenders of freedom become calumniators, the rebels were friends of truth and defenders of oppressed innocence. . . . " Robespierre concludes: "Louis must die in order that the country live." In selling his people to foreign despots, the king nullified the social pact that bound the nation together. Since then a state of war has been in effect between the people and the tyrant; the tyrant is to be destroyed as one destroys an enemy. Such is the point of view of the Revolution; it will make possible the consolidation of a republican order.

But these are considerations that in no way enter into Sade's thinking. When the blade severs the head of Louis XVI, it is in Sade's eyes not the citizen Capet, or even the traitor, who dies. It is, in his eyes as in those of Joseph de Maistre and of all the Ultramontanists, the representative of God who dies. And it is the blood of the temporal representative of God, and in a deeper sense, the blood of God, that falls back upon the heads of the people in insurrection. Catholic counterrevolutionary philosophers such as Joseph de Maistre, Bonald, and Maine de Biran speak of the putting to death of Louis XVI as a redemptive martyrdom; for them Louis expiates the sins of the nation. For Sade, the putting to death of the king plunges the nation into the inexpiable; the regicides are parricides. Sade doubtless saw in the inexpiable a coercive force; he then wished to substitute for the fraternity of the natural man the solidarity of the parricide, the solidarity of a community that could not be fraternal because it is of Cain.

4. From Society without God to Society without Executioner

The Revolution wishes to establish fraternity and equality among the children of the mother fatherland [*la mère patrie*]. What a strange expression, the mother fatherland! It implies a hermaphrodite divinity whose ambiguous nature seems to convey the complexity of the putting to death of the king. The expression comes from the ambivalence of the revolutionary act, an ambivalence which the men of the Convention clearly could not be aware of but which they take into account by substituting the mother fatherland for the sacred instance of the father, that is, the king. But could in fact the slaves in revolt—who by their revolt against their masters have made themselves accomplices in the revolt of their masters against God in order to become masters in their turn—claim to found a community of innocents? To become innocent, they would have to expiate the inexpiable putting to death of the king. All they can do is push the consummation of evil to its extreme limits. In his address on the trial of the king, Robespierre says:

> When a nation has been forced to resort to the right to insurrection, it enters into the state of nature with regard to the tyrant. How then could the tyrant invoke the social pact? He has nullified it. The nation can still preserve the

social pact if it judges it to be in force in what concerns the
citizens among themselves. But the effect of tyranny and insurrection is to break entirely with the tyrant; it is to constitute tyranny and insurrection in a state of war with one
another. The tribunals and juridical procedures are made
only for the members of the city.

It is here that the crucial point of divergence between Sade
and the Revolution, Sade and the Terror, Sade and Robespierre,
can be seen. Once the tyrant has been annihilated, can the social
pact exist unilaterally for the citizens among themselves? Can the
tribunals and juridical procedures continue to exist for the members of the city? Sade replies: How could they? You have revolted
against iniquity. For you iniquity consisted in being excluded from
the practice of iniquity. In revolting against iniquity you have an-
swered only with iniquity, since as your masters had killed God in
their consciousness, you have killed your masters. If you are not to
return to servitude, justice, for you—and you have given bloody
proofs of this—can consist only in the common practice of individual iniquity. How will you appeal, if not to God, at least to an identified order that will secure for you the tranquil enjoyment of the
benefits of the insurrection? Everything you undertake will henceforth bear the mark of assassination.

This Sade sets out to demonstrate in his tract entitled "Yet
Another Effort, Frenchmen, If You Would be Republicans"—
which is not so much his as that of Dolmancé, one of the characters
in Sade's *Philosophy in the Bedroom*, in which this tract is inserted.
Still, since we have good reasons to think that it is in his fiction that
he expressed what was at the bottom of his thinking (if this thinking
has a bottom to it), we must assign more importance to this strange
document than to the many protestations of republican civic con-
victions with which he gratified the revolutionary authorities during his nine years of freedom.

Already the declamatory title—"Yet Another Effort,
Frenchmen . . . "—appears suspect indeed and gives us enough of

a glimpse into the real intentions of the author. There are two chapters: the first devoted to religion, the second to morals. In the first chapter, in which he seeks to demonstrate that theism in no way suits a republican government, Sade uses positive rational arguments to undermine the bases of theocratic society. The issue is put in these terms: Christianity must be rejected because its social consequences are immoral; atheism alone can ensure an ethical basis for national education.

> Rather than fatigue your children's young organs with deific stupidities, replace them with excellent social principles; instead of teaching them futile prayers . . . , let them be instructed in their duties toward society; train them to cherish the virtues you scarcely ever mentioned in former times and which, without your religious fables, are sufficient for their individual happiness; make them sense that this happiness consists in rendering others as fortunate as we desire to be ourselves. If you base these truths upon Christian chimeras, as you so foolishly used to do, scarcely will your pupils have detected the absurd futility of its foundations than they will overthrow the entire edifice, and they will become bandits for the simple reason they believe the religion they have toppled forbids them to be bandits. On the other hand, if you make them sense the necessity of virtue, because their happiness depends upon it, egoism will turn them into honest people, and this law which dictates their behavior to men will always be the surest, the soundest of all. (*PB*, 303–4)

These are positive materialist principles that at first sight seem rationally irrefutable and capable of supplying the bases for a new society. They can give rise to would-be bold innovations such as the suppression of the family, the authorization of free unions— that is, the community of men for women and the community of women for men—and especially the nationalization of children, who will know no father but the state. All these problems are raised by Sade (we could see here a foreshadowing of some of Fourier's ideas for the phalanstery); we next see his solutions. In the second chapter, devoted to morals, he immediately drives "Republicans" into a corner:

> In according freedom of conscience and of the press, consider, citizens—for it is practically the same thing—whether freedom of action must not be granted too: excepting direct clashes with the underlying principles of government, there remain to you it is impossible to say how many fewer crimes to punish, because in fact there are very few criminal actions in a society whose foundations are liberty and equality. (*PB*, 307)

Can individual happiness really consist in rendering others as fortunate as we desire to be ourselves—as atheist morality had claimed? "The point is not at all to love our brethren as oneself," the second chapter immediately answers, spelling out the first consequences of atheist morality, "since that is in defiance of all the laws of Nature, and since hers is the sole voice which must direct all the actions of our life" (*PB*, 309). Set up a community of women for men and a community of men for women—but in order to fill the public palaces of national prostitution. A community of children? To be sure—to make them the more available for sodomy. The suppression of the family? Certainly, but with an exception that proves the rule: incest. The community of wealth? Through theft, for "by what right will he who has nothing be enchained by an agreement which protects only him who has everything?" (*PB*, 313). "Punish the man neglectful enough to let himself be robbed; but proclaim no kind of penalty against robbery. Consider whether your pledge does not authorize the act, and whether he who commits it does any more than put himself in harmony with the most sacred of Nature's movements, that of preserving one's own existence at no matter whose expense" (*PB*, 314). But if calumny, theft, rape, incest, adultery, and sodomy are not to be sanctioned in a republican government, the crime which this government is least justified to punish is murder.

It has been pointed out that there are certain virtues whose practice is impossible for certain men, just as there are certain remedies which do not agree with certain constitutions. Now, would it not be to carry your injustice beyond all limits were you to send the law to strike the man incapable of bowing to the law? . . . From these first principles there follows, one feels, the necessity to make flexible, mild laws and especially to get rid forever of the atrocity of capital punishment, . . . since the law, cold and impersonal, is a total stranger to the passions which are able to justify in man the cruel act of murder. Man receives his impressions from Nature, who is able to forgive him this act; the law, on the contrary, always opposed as it is to Nature and receiving nothing from her, cannot be authorized to permit itself the same extravagances; not having the same motives, the law cannot have the same rights. (*PB*, 310).

A government that was born from the murder of God and that continues to exist through murder has lost in advance the right to inflict capital punishment; it consequently could not pronounce sanction against any other crime: "The republic being permanently menaced from the outside by the despots surrounding it . . . will preserve itself only by war, and nothing is less moral than war" (*PB*, 315). Is [murder] a political crime? We must avow, on the contrary, that it is, unhappily, merely one of policy's and politics' greatest instruments. Is it not by dint of murders that France is free today? . . . "What study, what science, has greater need of murder's support than that which tends only to deceive, whose sole end is the expansion of one nation at another's expense? . . . Strange blindness in man, who publicly teaches the art of killing, who rewards the most accomplished killer, and who punishes him who for some particular reason does away with his enemy!" (*PB*, 332). " 'I grant you pardon,' said Louis XV to Charolais, who, to divert himself, had just killed a man; 'but I also pardon whoever will kill you.' All the bases of the law against murderers may be found in that sublime motto" (*PB*, 337). We see here Sade recall

quite opportunely the principles that governed life in the old monarchy, whose immorality the Republic is only to consecrate:

> I ask how one will be able to demonstrate that in a state
> rendered *immoral* by its obligations, it is essential that the
> individual be *moral?* I will go further: it is a very good thing
> he is not. . . . Insurrection . . . is not at all a *moral* condi-
> tion; however, it has got to be a republic's permanent con-
> dition. Hence it would be no less absurd than dangerous to
> require that those who are to ensure the perpetual *immoral*
> subversion of the established order themselves be *moral* be-
> ings; for the state of a moral man is one of tranquillity and
> peace, the state of an *immoral* man is one of perpetual un-
> rest that pushes him to, and identifies him with, the neces-
> sary insurrection in which the republican must always keep
> the government of which he is a member. (*PB*, 315)

At the beginning of his tract, Sade affirmed that with atheism
one would inculcate in children excellent social principles. Then he
draws out, one after another, the consequences that follow from
these principles: they will throw society into a state of perpetual
movement, a state of permanent immorality—that is, throw society
ineluctably into its own destruction.

5

In other words, the vision of a society in the state of permanent
immorality presents itself as a *utopia of evil.* And this paradoxical
utopia corresponds to the virtual state of our modern society. But
while the utopian sense of human possibilities elaborates the anticipations of a virtual progress, the sadist mind elaborates the anticipations of a virtual regression. These anticipations are the more
hallucinatory in that the method is put to the service of regression.
However, unlike the utopias of good which sin by leaving the evil
realities out of account, the utopia of evil leaves out of account, not

the possibilities of good, but that important factor which is ennui. For if ennui most often breeds evil, once evil is done the ennui still increases; just as disgust follows crime when it has been committed for the sole purpose of committing a crime. Sade retains only the evil realities, while suppressing their temporal character. Then evil alone fills each moment of social life and destroys each moment with the next. The utopia of a society in the state of permanent criminality is something conceived in Sade's ennui and disgust. Were it to be taken literally, and were the ideologues of evil to put it into practice, this utopian society would sink ineluctably into disgust and ennui. Against disgust and ennui there can be no remedy save to go yet further into new crimes ad infinitum.[3]

6

We can imagine here, underlying the Revolution, a sort of moral conspiracy whose goal would have been to force an idle humanity, which had lost the sense of its social necessity, to become conscious of its guilt. This conspiracy would have used two methods: an exoteric method practiced by Joseph de Maistre in his sociology of original sin, and an infinitely complex esoteric method that dons the mask of atheism in order to combat atheism, that speaks the language of moral skepticism in order to combat moral skepticism, solely in order to credit reason with all it can give so as to demonstrate its nullity.

As we read on in Sade's tract, we are the more perplexed. We are tempted to wonder if Sade did not wish to discredit in his own way the immortal principles of 1789; if this disestablished great lord did not espouse the philosophy of the Enlightenment solely in order to reveal the darkness of its foundations.

Here we find again the questions we had at the beginning. On the one hand, we could take Sade literally, in which case he appears to us as one of the most searching and most revealing epiphenomena of a vast process of social decomposition and recomposition. He would then be shown to be like an abscess on a sick body which thought it was authorized to speak in the name of this body. His political nihilism would be but what one calls an unhealthy episode of the collective process; his apology for pure crime, his invitation to persevere in crime, would be but the attempt to pervert the political instinct, that is, the collectivity's instinct for self-preservation. For with profound satisfaction the people exterminate those who have opposed them; the collectivity always senses what is, wrongly or rightly, harmful to it. That is why it can confound, with the greatest conviction, cruelty and justice without experiencing the least remorse. The rites it can invent at the foot of the scaffold free it from pure cruelty; it knows how to disguise cruelty's form and effects.

The other alternative is that we can stop at certain passages that make this kind of declaration:

> Let no one tax me with being a dangerous innovator; let no one say that by my writings I seek to blunt the remorse in evildoers' hearts, that my humane ethics are wicked because they augment those same evildoers' penchant for crime. I wish formally to certify here and now that I have none of these perverse intentions; I set forth the ideas which, since the age when I first began to reason, have identified themselves in me, and to whose expression and realization the infamous despotism of tyrants has been opposed for uncounted centuries. So much the worse for those susceptible to corruption by any idea; so much the worse for them who fasten upon naught but the harmful in philosophic opinions, who are likely to be corrupted by everything. Who knows? They may have been poisoned by reading Seneca and Charron. It is not to them I speak; I address myself only to people capable of hearing me out, and they will read me without any danger. (PB, 311)

A supreme degree of consciousness shows itself here, one that can encompass the entire process of decomposition and recomposition. Then, while recognizing in Sade his role of executor, we must also attribute to him the function of denouncing the dark forces camouflaged as social values by the defense mechanisms of the collectivity. Thus camouflaged, these dark forces can dance their infernal round in the void. Sade was not afraid to get involved with these forces, but he enters into the dance only in order to tear off the masks that the Revolution had put on them to make them acceptable and to allow the "children of the fatherland" to embody these dark forces with innocence.

Outline
of
Sade's System

Without claiming to retrace here the chronological development of Sade's thought, we shall try as far as possible to outline the different phases of its dialectical process and decipher the different layers of an experience that has remained obscure. In doing so, we shall respect Sade's terminology and, taking him literally, shall seek to make explicit the system this terminology implies and delineates. But to what extent is this terminology really his?

Magnetized by the events that are getting underway outside (the assault on the principles of religious and social authority), dark forces arise within a man, who then feels himself forced to declare them to his contemporaries, even though he must live among them as a moral smuggler. If he does not set out to invent a language appropriate to these forces, a language that would make them comprehensible if not to his contemporaries at least to posterity, he will have to express himself in the accepted terminology, that is, with the current philosophical entities. Thus, in the philosophical systems with which the characters in his books speculate, Sade draws on the rationalism of Voltaire and the Encyclopedists and on the materialism of d'Holbach and La Mettrie. And his characters move with perfect ease from one system to another under the dictates of their passions, with scarcely any concern for the contradictions that result. Sade wishes to show by this that it is temperament that inspires the choice of a philosophy, and that reason itself, which the

philosophers of his time invoked, is but a form of passion. Thus he
interchangeably names his characters devotees of virtue, devotees of
vice, and therefore also devotees of reason. But on the whole, Sade
appears no less a prisoner of the terminology of his century than he
was bodily a prisoner of the different political regimes of his time. A
prisoner in the name of the king by lettre de cachet, then a prisoner
in the name of the law by the will of the people, he was even more a
prisoner in the name of reason and the philosophy of the Enlightenment, because he wished to translate into the terms of common
sense what common sense must pass over in silence and abolish in
order to remain common, lest it be itself abolished. In Sade's time it
is taken as understood that religion is an enterprise of mystification
and that human actions have no other motive than self-interest.
These are the two conclusions the thought of the end of the century
had come to; this thought does away with the soul by discrediting, in
the name of the idea of self-interest, all contrary capacities—effu-
sions, sufferings for another, sacrifice—which flow from generosity
and the richness of being. The mechanist explanation of man and of
nature then becomes the sole valid one. From this current thinking
Sade makes essential its fundamental criterion, *suspicion*—which is
also one of the dominant traits of his own character. I am being
deceived? Then I must deceive. Others are dissimulating? Then I
must dissimulate. Others are pretending and masking themselves?
Give us simulacra and masks. But it turns out that the best mask, the
best simulacrum, is the accepted terminology of common sense. We
have said that Sade had at his disposal no other terminology and
dialectics than those of the philosophy of the Enlightenment; this is
why many today find him unreadable. But Sade, with his habitual
violence, will make this language convey all it is capable of convey-
ing; he will push the mechanist explanation of man to the point of
delirium, and he will show its practical application in the hands of
precisely those whom common sense disowns. In this way he will
reveal the absurdity of the mechanist psychology of his time and denounce its mendacity: it is not out of self-interest but to the contrary

without the least concern for his own self-interest that man can act as we are pleased to describe him. And even when man thinks he is consciously obeying only his own egoism, in this case too he will always obey forces impenetrable to reason alone. Richer than he dared think, he will, if necessary, display a sinister generosity and sacrifice. No doubt Sade seems for a moment to agree with the determinism of the mechanists when, following the philosophical marching orders of his age, he says that man could not act otherwise. But he forthwith refutes their system, which situates, crudely, the lack of freedom in physiological reflexes, when he depicts for us man in those strange ways of acting and feeling that perversion commands. This is why, from his time to ours, he has been thought not only unreadable but repugnant. Indeed, it is in the capacity to imagine monstrous reflexes ad infinitum that man, deprived as he is of freedom, nonetheless appears to be in search of a freedom he has lost, a freedom his power to imagine makes him aware of and substitutes for. And if this loss of original freedom leaves him subject to dark forces, these forces, when they occupy the imagination, indicate also what had originally been possessed and is now lost. But this indication remains no less obscure than those forces, which for their part are irreducible to any rational explanation. Materialists and mechanists have thought that in their general system of nature and man they could reduce the irreducible phenomenon that Sade believed he had to revive. What is more, the materialist or mechanist system is in the final analysis only the expression of a mind that accepts the moral eclipse that follows this loss of inward freedom just in the measure that it seeks to compensate for it by external freedom in the social sphere. Now the perspective changes for us; it is not Sade who appears as a disciple of the mechanists and materialists, but their systems appear to be at the service of those forces that Sade both incarnates and denounces.

The Marquis de Sade grew up in a society that was aware that it rested on arbitrariness. The moral malaise of this society, which had everything to fear from the extreme cynicism of some of its representatives, is what is at the origin of Sade's philosophical preoccupations. These preoccupations convey first a state of bad conscience, the bad conscience of the libertine great lord, which is more demanding in Sade since he suffers the pressure of the irrational forces in his own personality. A deep need for justification leads Sade to seek arguments for his defense in the philosophy of La Mettrie or d'Holbach, and, even better, of Spinoza.

If the court trials and condemnations that his different outbursts provoke, in particular in Arcueil and Marseilles; his repeated incarcerations; finally his long detention by lettre de cachet instigated by his mother-in-law[1]—if all this arbitrary repression necessarily makes him, the apologist for the arbitrary, rise in revolt against every institution, every law "human or divine," are we to see in that anything but the outward projection of his inward trial, that which his own conscience conducts against him? Perhaps the iniquitous punishment his unconscious brings upon him is necessary to him, in order to win acquittal in his inward trial.

Does adherence to materialist atheism break down the human morality contained in the maxim: Let us not do to others what we would not want them to do to us? Does not the denial of God involve the denial of the neighbor? Such seems to be the initial problem that Sade addresses, when, arbitrarily shut up by the justice of men, he stands before the tribunal of his conscience. But he will ask further: When the existence of God, that is, the judge, is denied, what becomes of the culprit?

In the *Dialogue between a Priest and a Dying Man*, composed in 1782, he writes:

> Prove to me that matter is inert and I will grant you a creator, prove to me that Nature does not suffice to herself.
> . . . Your god is a machine you fabricated in your passions' behalf, you manipulated it to their liking; but the day it interfered with mine, I kicked it out of my way. . . . Good friends and on the best terms have we ever been, this soul

and I, so Nature wished it to be; as it is, so she expressly
modeled it, for my soul is the result of the dispositions she
formed in me pursuant to her own ends and needs; and as
she has an equal need of vices and of virtues, whenever she
was pleased to move to evil, she did so, whenever she
wanted a good deed from me, she roused in me the desire
to perform one, and even so I did as I was bid. Look no-
where but to her workings for the unique cause of our
fickle human behavior. . . . [2]

The serenity of this conscience is reflected in the beauty of style of
this dialogue. But when this conscience says, "It is then possible
that things necessarily come about without being determined by a
superior intelligence, and possible hence that everything derives
logically from a primary cause, without there being either reason
or wisdom in that primary cause" (169), does this conscience realize how heavy with the approaching storms is this sentence? In any
case, for this apparently so serene conscience, "reason alone
should warn us that harm done to our fellows can never bring happiness to us; and our heart, that contributing to their felicity is the
greatest joy Nature has accorded us on earth; the entirety of human morals is contained in this one phrase: *Render others as happy as
one desires oneself to be,* and never inflict more pain upon them than
one would like to receive at their hands" (174). These passages
show clearly that Sade still believes in the possibility of maintaining
moral categories without drawing out the consequences that can
result from the nonexistence of God. But five years later he composes the first version of *Justine,* then entitled *The Misfortunes of
Virtue,* and he comments on it in these terms: "A work of a quite
new taste; from one end to the other vice triumphs and virtue is
humiliated. The denouement alone renders to virtue all the luster
due it. No one who finishes reading this book fails to abhor the
false triumph of crime and cherish the humiliations of virtue."[3]
This marginal note to the first version of the "infamous *Justine*"
written five years after the *Dialogue* bears witness to the violence of

the conflict that has begun in Sade and shows that his mind has entered into a dialectical drama that will perhaps last his lifetime. In *The Misfortunes of Virtue*—as the first version was entitled—not only are moral categories maintained, but Christian categories reappear. These, however, will serve only as the basis for the development of the thought of the work; they will be discussed and refuted by the characters whom the virtuous heroine encounters in the course of her adventures. This version of *Justine* thus seems to be the egg from which Sade's philosophy will hatch; the still-moral mind is but the shell that will break under the pressure of the dialectical germination of the problems that this mind puts to itself. Yet, if this work already contains the elements of the anarchist philosophy of the later versions, it still presents itself as an illustration of the fundamental dogma of Christianity, that of *the reversibility of the merits of sacrifice of the innocent in favor of the guilty*. This dogma Joseph de Maistre will take up twenty years later in his *Saint Petersburg Nights*. Still later, Sade and Maistre reappear together in the sensibility of their fraternal reader Baudelaire.

Thus the misfortunes of Justine, far from being judged to be "things that come about necessarily without there being any wisdom in them," are seen by Juliette—who will later be the heroine of *The Prosperities of Vice*—as so many enigmas of Providence. When, to add to all her adversities, the bolt of lightning strikes Justine dead before the eyes of her sister, Juliette, Juliette, whose whole career was made in vice, sees in this final blow a warning from Heaven:

> The unheard of sufferings this luckless creature has experienced although she has always respected her duties, have something about them which is too extraordinary for me not to open my eyes upon my own self; think not I am blinded by that false-gleaming felicity which, in the course of Therese's adventures, we have seen enjoyed by the villains who battened upon her. These caprices of Heaven's hand are enigmas it is not for us to sound, but which ought

> never seduce us. O thou my friend! The prosperity of Crime
> is but an ordeal to which Providence would expose Virtue,
> it is like the lightning whose deceptive fires embellish the at-
> mosphere for a moment only to hurl into the abysses of
> death the unhappy one they dazzle.[4]

What are we to think of the state of mind in which Sade found himself, when, five years after the *Dialogue,* he composed these pages of a quasi-Jansenist inspiration, pages not completely exterior to a certain Augustinianism? In the light of the comments cited above, the significance of the conclusion here seems to go well beyond that of a simple literary maneuver. At least we refuse to believe that Sade would have wished to cast a Christian veil over his own philosophy. If it were but a veil, this veil would also exist in his own mind and all his audacities would not have rent it. This tormented mind, one of the most profound of his age, was no doubt subject to powerful oscillations.

The first version of *Justine* marks a stage in the evolution of the Sadean consciousness. The problem of evil is formulated in all rigor and in a quasi-theological form. First denied in the *Dialogue* along with the existence of God, and, perhaps, intellectually resolved, the problem remains intact in *The Misfortunes of Virtue.* About the same time, Sade was already conceiving the plan for his first great work, *The 120 Days of Sodom,*[5] whose prodigious architecture will be unequaled in his subsequent works. This work lays the foundations for a theory of perversions and prepares the metaphysics developed especially in *Juliette.* In it we find the exact definition of the problem of evil in the Sadean mind: the misfortune of *being virtuous in crime and finding oneself criminal in the practice of virtue.* If Sade at first held to the denial of evil, he is not yet satisfied with this negation. The reason is that the neighbor is found to be involved, and as long as the neighbor exists for the ego, he reveals the presence of God. In the subsequent versions of *Justine*[6] and in *The Story of Juliette,* the resolution of the notion of evil will go through several phases and take several forms: now that of a destructive theology born from the bad conscience of the libertine great lord; now that of an atheist, materialist, Stoic, and asocial naturalism (theory of pure crime); now that of an ascesis, the ascesis of apathy.

When did Sade personally come out of this "problematic" period? We have grounds to suppose that when he was writing *The Story of Juliette,* that is, during his years of freedom between 1790 and 1798, he had gone through all the phases. But it is not possible for us today to determine if he ever accomplished the *affective* resolution of evil in himself.

1

In Sade's work the bad conscience of the debauched libertine represents a transitional state of mind between the conscience of the social man and the atheistic mind of the philosopher of Nature. The libertine's behavior presents negative elements that Sade's thought, in its dialectical movement, will try to eliminate, and along with them, positive elements that will make it possible to move beyond this intermediary state of mind and arrive at the atheist and asocial philosophy of Nature, the morality of perpetual motion.

The libertine mind maintains a negative relationship with God, on the one hand, and with the neighbor, on the other. Both the notion of God and that of the neighbor are indispensable to it.

The negative relationship with God is indispensable: the libertine mind, we could say with Sade, is not "coldly" atheist; it is atheist through its effervescence, therefore out of resentment. Its atheism is but a form of sacrilege. Only the profanation of the symbols of religion can make its apparent atheism convincing to itself. In this it is clearly distinguishable from the mind of the atheist philosopher, for which sacrilege has no other significance than that of revealing the weakness of the one who indulges in it.[7]

At times the atheism that the libertine mind affects and the

offenses whose execution it conceives are put forth as provocations
addressed to the absent God, as though scandal were a means to
force God to manifest his existence.

> Were there a God and were this God to have any power,
> would he permit the virtue which honors him, and which
> you profess, to be sacrificed to vice and libertinage as it is
> going to be? Would this all-powerful God permit a feeble
> creature like myself, who would, face to face with him, be as
> a mite in the eye of an elephant, would he, I say, permit this
> feeble creature to insult him, to flout him, to defy him, to
> challenge him, to offend him as I do, wantonly, at my own
> sweet will, at every instant of the day?[8]

Impunity adds to the delectation of this kind of mind; the greater
the punishment deserved, the more valuable the offense is in its
eyes. Remorse is always active in this mind and seems to be the
motive for the crime. For the debauched libertine it is, not an action taken by the atheist philosopher to be morally indifferent because it is determined by perpetual motion, but evil that will be the
essential goal of the extension of the sphere of gratifications.
"What animates us is not the object of libertinage, but rather the
idea of evil." The object of libertinage would be of no interest if it
did not make one do further evil. Not only is the possibility of doing good not excluded, but this possibility gives crime all its value.
Thus in thinking it is able to do evil, the mind of the debauched
sadist maintains, along with moral categories, its free will. The
mind of the debauched libertine, as Sade sees it, not only appears
here in complete apposition to atheism but has a relationship with
the analysis of evil for the sake of evil which we find in Saint Augustine's *Confessions*.

Such a mind is consequently able to elaborate a complete destructive theology like that of the religion of the Being Supreme in
Wickedness,[9] the only theology that Saint-Fond, the perfect exem-
plar of the libertine and debauched great lord, would want to

profess. This religion of evil does not yet consist in denying crime, as the philosophy of perpetual motion will, but consists in admitting crime as proceeding from the existence of an infernal God. It is not the refutation of the dogma of the necessity of the sacrifice of the innocent for the salvation of the guilty—the thesis of the first version of *Justine*—but the reverse of that dogma: it exalts the necessity of injustice in God. For, confronted with the mystery of Revelation, scandalized reason, if it wishes to state the dogma of that mystery in the language of scandal, can substitute for the revealed content only a blasphemous content that will be the exact expression of the impression that mystery makes on reason abandoned to itself. Then, before crime on the one hand and sufferings on the other, it imputes to orthodoxy the claim to legitimate the crimes of the guilty by expiation, the expiatory virtue of the sufferings of the innocent. In fact, orthodoxy attributes crime to the freedom to sin and attributes to the sufferings of the innocent the virtue of expiating crime. What scandalized reason imputes to orthodoxy is precisely what it itself will state as a doctrine. This doctrine will appear to have the merit of being founded on the supernatural origin of sin, but the conclusions it draws will be the opposite of those of orthodoxy: Would not all the evils with which God afflicts humanity be the ransom God exacts before granting man the right to make others suffer and be infinitely vicious? Then one could see in God the original culprit who attacked man before man attacked him; from this, man would have acquired the right and the strength to attack his fellow. And this divine aggression would be so incommensurable that it would legitimate the impunity of the guilty one and the sacrifice of the innocent.

> If the misfortunes that afflict me from the day I am born
> until the day I die prove his indifference to me, I may very
> well be mistaken upon what I call *evil*. What I thus charac-
> terize relative to myself seems indeed to be a very great
> good relative to the being who has brought me into the
> world; and if I receive *evil* from others, I enjoy the right to

pay them back in kind, to be the first to cast the stone: so, henceforth, *evil* is good, just as it is for the author of my existence, relatively to my existence: the *evil* I do others makes me happy, as God is rendered happy by the *evil* he does me. (*J*, 396)

Evil "is, however, a moral entity and not a created one, an eternal and not a perishable entity: it existed before the world; it constituted the monstrous, the execrable being who was able to fashion such a hideous world" (*J*, 400). This evil can sustain the universe only through evil, can perpetuate it only for evil, and permits creation to exist only inasmuch as it is impregnated with evil.

> All, everyone has got to be wicked, barbarous, inhuman, like your God: these are the vices the person who wishes to please him must adopt, without, nevertheless, any hope of succeeding: for the *evil* which harms always, the *evil* which is the essence of God, will never be, can never be susceptible of love nor of gratitude. If this God, center of *evil* and of ferocity, torments man and has him tormented by Nature and by other men throughout the whole period of his existence, how may one doubt that he acts likewise and perhaps involuntarily upon this breath of air which outlives him and which . . . is nothing other than *evil* itself? (*J*, 397)

What then has become of the good being?

> He whom you call virtuous is not by any means good, or, if he is from your viewpoint, he surely is not from the viewpoint of God, who is only *evil*, who wants nothing but what is *evil*, who requires *evil* alone. The man you speak of is merely feeble, and feebleness is an *evil*. Weaker than the absolutely and entirely vicious being, . . . this man will have to suffer a great deal more. . . . The more vices and crimes a man would have manifested in this world, the more he will be in harmony with his ineluctable fate, which is wickedness, which I consider the primary matter of the world's composition. (*J*, 398)

Thus, "far from denying God as the atheist does, or washing him of his offenses as the deist does," the mind of the debauched libertine agrees to admit God with all his vices. The existence of evil in the world gives this mind the means to blackmail God, the eternally Guilty Party because the original Aggressor, and for this end it always resorts to moral categories as to a pact that God has violated. Suffering becomes a bill of exchange made out on God.

Thus this mind also has to establish a negative relationship with the neighbor: "The *evil* I do others makes me happy, as God is rendered happy by the *evil* he does me." This mind then derives its gratification from its continual opposition to the notion of the love of one's neighbor, an opposition it uses in its theory of the *pleasure of comparison*. One of the four debauchees in *The 120 Days of Sodom* says:

> There is one essential thing lacking to our happiness. It is the pleasure of comparison, a pleasure which can only be born of the sight of wretched persons, and here one sees none at all. It is from the sight of him who does not in the least enjoy what I enjoy, and who suffers, that comes the charm of being able to say to oneself: "I am therefore happier than he." Wherever men may be found equal, and where these differences do not exist, happiness shall never exist either: it is the story of the man who only knows full well what health is worth after he has been ill. (362)

How, then, is one to relieve the wretched?

> The voluptuousness I sense and which is the result of this sweet comparison of their condition with mine, would cease to exist were I to succor them. . . . One should in one way or another, so as the better to establish that distinction indispensable to happiness, one should, I say, rather aggravate their plight.

Thus, while the atheist mind will denounce moral categories as fabricated by the weak, the consciousness of the debauched libertine is content to remain within the sphere of those categories, which it inverts. Yet through the need for comparison, the strong man is putting into question his own strength; by comparing his situation with that of the wretched, the fortunate man ineluctably identifies himself with the wretched one. In torturing the object of his lusts in order to derive pleasure from his suffering, the debauchee will represent to himself his own suffering, his own being tortured, and in so doing will also represent his own punishment. Saint-Fond, after having outrageously mistreated a family of poor people, is taken in a fake surprise attack by two men whom he himself has ordered to flagellate him. Thus the fear he inspired in the weak will become his own fear in the representation of the strong: "I love to make them experience the sort of thing that troubles and over-whelms my existence so cruelly." At this stage, the mind thus re-mains riveted on the reality of the other, which it seeks to deny but only makes more intense by the love-hate it discharges on the other. The debauchee remains attached to the victim of his lusts, and to the individuality of this victim, whose sufferings he would like to prolong "beyond the limits of eternity—if eternity there be." The true atheist, to the extent that he really exists, does not attach himself to any object; caught up in the perpetual motion of nature, he obeys his impulses and looks upon nature's creatures as no more than its foam. The mind of the debauched libertine can-not renounce its human, all-too-human, aspirations; only the Stoic atheist could. Thus it remains not only obsessed by the neighbor as a victim but also haunted by the idea of death. It cannot renounce the singular hope for a future, infernal, life, that is, it cannot con-sent to the annihilation of its "body of sin," because of its mad desire eternally to hurl its furies upon the same victim (*J*, 369).

But in this phase, this consciousness of the debauched liber-tine, inasmuch as it represents one of the moments of Sade's own consciousness, betrays an obscure need for expiation. If this need could be elucidated, such expiation would have no other meaning but that of a liquidation of self, a freeing from the self done by oneself. Such are the positive themes of this consciousness. The need for expiation is in this consent to undergo eternal damnation. No doubt, it consents in order to gloat over the sufferings of its victim; yet the consent does imply the desire to share these sufferings.

The character of Saint-Fond reveals still another characteristic trait of the libertine mind: pride over its condition, contempt for its fellowman, and hatred, mixed with fear, of "that vile mob they call the people." All the components of this haughty attitude go with humiliating practices of debauchery, contrived to shock the people's morality: "Only minds organized like ours know how well the humiliation imposed by certain wanton acts serves as pride's nourishment." In effect, what the popular, or rather bourgeois, mentality could not admit or understand is that those it considers the guardians of the social order could, by their own voluntary degradation, challenge the social order, and in so doing overturn all social values. In this humiliation—though it be only fictitious in the sadist libertine—there is also manifest a need for willful debasement and, in this need, the feeling of right that the idea of one's superiority confers: the right to revise the notion of man in one's individual self, an *experimental right,* which it would be dangerous to grant to common mortals. The exercise of this *right to forbidden experiments*, born from the libertine consciousness, will form one of the fundamental commitments of the Sadean consciousness.

2

> When it wants martyrs, atheism has only to say the word; my blood is ready to flow.
>
> —*The New Justine*, vol. 1

Let us now consider the characteristic features of Sade's materialist atheism, such as it appears in the works written in the decade after the *Dialogue.* Never again will Sade express himself in the serene style of that tract. The materialists and the Encyclopedists, Sade's contemporaries, when they admit matter in the state of perpetual motion as the universal agent that excludes any need for the existence of a god, imply that knowledge of the laws governing this matter will make possible a better individual and social morality, as well as an unlimited rational exploitation of Nature by man. But when the arguments of La Mettrie, Helvétius, and d'Holbach come into contact with Sade's thought, they undergo an unforeseen development. For Sade, the substitution of Nature in the state of perpetual motion for God signifies, not the arrival of a happier era for humanity, but only the beginning of tragedy and its conscious and deliberate acceptance. We can see here an anticipation of the Nietzschean theme that opposes to the sufferings of the innocent a conscience that agrees to suffer its guilt because it feels itself existing only at this price. This is the hidden meaning of Sade's atheism, which differentiates him so clearly from his contemporaries. To admit matter in the state of perpetual motion as the one and only universal agent is equivalent to consenting to live as an individual in a state of perpetual motion.

> As soon as a body appears to have lost motion by its passage
> from the state of life to what is improperly called death, it
> tends, from that very moment, toward dissolution; yet disso-
> lution is a very great state of motion. There is, therefore, no
> moment when the body of the animal is at rest; it never
> dies; but because it no longer exists for us, we believe that it
> no longer exists at all. Bodies are transmuted . . . metamor-
> phosed, but they are never inert. Inertia is absolutely impos-
> sible for matter whether matter is organized or not. Weigh
> these truths carefully and you will see where they lead and
> what a twist they give to human morality.

Once having reached this position, on the threshold of the unknown, Sade's thought, looking back upon itself, steps back, scandalized by its own inevitable conclusions. Then we see this

82

SADE MY NEIGHBOR

thought take hold of itself and accept its discoveries. Thus the atheist and materialist speeches of some of the characters in his works
strike us as so many moments of the efforts of his own thought to
get away from moral categories; this is what gives these speeches
their peculiarly dramatic tone. Is this matter perpetually in motion,
which trembles with pleasure and procures gratification only in dissolution and destruction, really blind and without will? Is there not
an intention in this universal agent?

We then look on the strange spectacle of Sade insulting Nature as he had insulted God. For Sade discovers in Nature the features of the God who creates the multitude of men for the purpose
of making them undergo everlasting tortures, "even though it
would have conformed more with goodness and with reason and
justice to create only stones and plants rather than to shape men
whose conduct could only bring endless chastisements." But what a
frightful situation Nature puts us in,

> since disgust with life becomes so strong in the soul that
> there is not a single man who would want to live again, even
> if such an offer were made on the day of his death . . . yes,
> I abhor nature; and I detest her because I know her well.
> Aware of her frightful secrets, I have fallen back on myself
> and I have felt . . . I have experienced a kind of pleasure in
> copying her foul deeds. What a contemptible and odious be-
> ing to make me see the daylight only in order to have me
> find pleasure in everything that does harm to my fellow
> men. *Eh quoi!* I had hardly been born . . . I had hardly quit
> my cradle when she drew me toward the very horrors which
> are her delight! This goes beyond corruption . . . it is an in-
> clination, a penchant. Her barbarous hand can only nourish
> evil; evil is her entertainment. Should I love such a mother?
> No; but I will imitate her, all the while detesting her. I shall
> copy her, as she wishes, but I shall curse her unceasingly.

These are the words of the chemist Almani, a character whose psychological makeup reflects marvelously one of the positions taken

by Sade's thought. Like the debauched libertine, the chemist Almani still works out his ideas within the sphere of moral categories. Evil seems to him to be the sole element in Nature, as it was for the mind of the debauched libertine the sole element in the "absent" God. And the criminal chemist likewise believes that the solution to the problem of evil is to do evil. Here too Sade's thought offers us only an attitude of purely human revolt, with no hope other than that of being able to remain in revolt. For the reproach addressed to Nature, even more than that addressed to God, is evidently destined to remain without response, and even without any psychic benefit, since it is addressed to an instance whose very notion excludes any idea of justification. The atheist spirit that hurls the anathema against Nature has thus wanted to render absurd the reproach that it cannot repress and that escapes it in spite of itself. This mind, though it accepts Nature as the supreme instance, has not yet given up the mechanism of moral categories, which, in its struggle with God, it judged necessary and useful, for with them it can make God the object of revenge. But once God is rejected, this vengeful maneuver is rendered without effect by perpetual motion. The notion of perpetual motion absorbs every idea of annihilation, which now becomes nothing but a modification of the forms of matter; man can then no longer reply with outrage to what he considers Nature's outrage. He finds himself to be unavenged.

In Almani's words we can see another factor now enter into Sade's thought. Evil figures in Almani's speech as a mere term to convey the effect of the natural dynamism with which the mind of the scientist identifies. We see, in Almani's resolve to copy the "foul deeds" of Nature, an attempt being sketched out at reconciliation with universal order, or rather with universal disorder. Though astonished indignation is still provoked, curiosity, the need to know, now manifest themselves. The mind tends more and more toward considering itself an integral part of Nature, the domain of its investigations. It discovers in natural phenomena no longer only blind and necessary laws but its own intentions. That is, it discovers a coincidence between its intentions and natural phenomena. Natural phenomena will appear to it as so many suggestions of what the mind feels it has a mission to bring into reality.

"Punishments are always proportionate to the crime, and crimes are always proportionate to the amount of knowledge possessed by the guilty one; the Flood presupposes extraordinary crimes, and these crimes presuppose knowledge infinitely greater than what we possess." These are Joseph de Maistre's comments on the subject of original sin. Let us take note of the notion of a knowledge-crime relationship; is it not singularly represented by Sade's thought, and especially by certain of his heroes? If knowledge ends by becoming a crime, what one calls crime must contain the key to knowledge. Then it is only by extending ever further the sphere of crime that the mind, arriving at those "extraordinary crimes," will recuperate lost knowledge, "knowledge infinitely greater than that which we possess."

3

In line with these intentions, Sade will push materialist atheism to the point where it takes on the form of a transcendental fatalism, such as we see in the *System of Nature* the Pope expounds at length to Juliette (*J,* 765ff.). Here Sade's thought resolutely breaks away from its human condition and seeks to integrate itself into a mythical cosmogony. This is apparently the only way for it to extricate itself from the trial in which it finds itself as much accused at the end as at the start, searching in vain for a judge to acquit it, after having withdrawn its competence from the moral tribunal of men.

Sade first admits the existence of an original and eternal Nature outside the three kingdoms of species and of creatures. "Let Nature become subject to other laws, these creatures resulting from the present laws will exist no more, under these different ones, but Nature will nonetheless still exist, although by different laws" (*J*, 766–67). The creatures, which are "neither good, nor beautiful, nor precious," are only the result of her blind laws. Nature then creates man despite herself; she creates the laws specially applicable to man and from that point on has no further power over him. At the beginning of the Pope's speech, this original Nature is viewed as being entirely distinct from the nature of man. But though man is no longer dependent on the original Nature, he still cannot escape from the laws that are proper to him, the laws of his self-preservation and multiplication. Those laws, however, are in no way necessary to Nature. This is already a first proof of man's irrelevance in the midst of the universe. Man could quadruple his kind or annihilate his species completely, and the universe would not be altered in the least. But now Sade sees this Nature become aware of the competitor her own movement has set up before her:

> If man destroys himself, he does wrong—in his own eyes.
> But that is not the view Nature takes of the thing. As she
> sees it, if he multiplies he does wrong, for he usurps from
> Nature the honor of a new phenomenon, creatures being
> the necessary result of her workings. If those creatures that
> are cast were not to propagate themselves, she would cast
> new entities and enjoy a faculty she has ceased to be able to
> exercise. (*J*, 767).

By multiplying, man, following a law inherent only in him, does decided harm to the natural phenomena that are within Nature's capacity. Foreseeing the conflict, Sade modifies his terminology to make it more accurate for the description of the process, which now turns into a drama: "If creatures destroy one another, they do well as regards Nature; for no obligation to reproduce has been imposed upon them, they have simply received the faculty to reproduce; turning to destruction, they cease exercising it, and give Nature the opportunity to resume the propagation from which she refrained so long as it was needless" (*J*, 767–68). Multiplication of the species is no longer taken to be a law from which a creature is unable to exempt himself; it is only a faculty in competition with Nature's original faculty. As the Pope goes on elaborating his description of the conflict, Nature, first admitted as obeying blind laws, is more and more revealed as intentional—as "creative evolution." Even better, Sade says explicitly that man, in propagating himself or in not destroying himself, binds Nature to the secondary laws of the species and deprives her of her most active power (*J*, 768).[10] Nature, if she thus finds herself the first slave of her own laws, seems now to be still more conscious of them and maintains still more impetuously her desire to break the chains of those laws.

> Ah, does she leave us in any doubt of the point to which
> our increase inconveniences her? Can we not tell how eager
> she would be to halt our multiplication and be delivered of
> its ill effects? . . . Thus it is that these murders our laws
> punish so sternly, these murders we suppose the greatest
> outrage that can be inflicted upon Nature, not only, as you
> very well see, do her no hurt and can do her none, but are
> in some sort instrumental to her, since she is a great murderess herself and since her single reason for murdering is
> to obtain, from the wholesale annihilation of cast creatures,
> the chance to recast them anew. The most wicked individual
> on earth, the most abominable, the most ferocious, the most
> barbarous, and the most indefatigable murderer is therefore
> but the spokesman of her desires, the vehicle of her will,
> and the surest agent of her caprices. (*J*, 768–69)

In these pages we see how far the Sadean mind has gone from the theology of the Being Supreme in Wickedness to come to this conception of Nature. We have first seen this mind accept the existence of God in order to declare God guilty and take advantage of God's eternal guilt; we have seen it then make this God one with a Nature no less ferocious, still situating itself from the point of view of moral categories. But this satanization of Nature only prepared for the liquidation of human categories. For the conception of Na-

ture as aspiring to renew her most active power marks a dehumanization of Sade's thought—a dehumanization that now takes on
the form of a singular metaphysics. If Sade, counter to what he
habitually affirms, now goes so far as to consider man to be entirely
distinct from Nature, it is in order to bring out more effectively a
profound discord between the notion of the human being and the
notion of the universe, and to explain how all the attempts he attributes to Nature to repossess her rights must be proportionate to
this discord. We might also see in all this Sade's will to separate
himself from solidarity with man by imposing on himself the cate-
gorical imperative of a cosmic tribunal that demands the annihilation of all that is human. No doubt, like Nature, slave to her own
laws, Sade hopes for his total liberation. But if, as is said in the
System of Pope Pius VI, Nature seeks thus to recuperate forces by
from time to time making whole populations perish through dis-
ease, cataclysms, war, discord, or the crimes of villains, in fact only
that secondary nature of the three kingdoms ruled by the laws of
perpetual metempsychosis profits from these destructions. And
when Nature sends forth great criminals or great scourges capable
of annihilating those three kingdoms, she commits only another act
of impotence. To bring about their disappearance Nature would
have to destroy herself totally, and she does not have that kind of
mastery.

> Thus, through his murderings the wicked man not only aids
> Nature to attain ends she will nonetheless never entirely
> achieve, but also aids even the laws the three kingdoms re-
> ceived at their original casting. I say original casting to facil-
> itate the intelligence of my system, for, there never having
> been any creation and Nature being timeless, the first cast-
> ing of a given being endures so long as that being's line sur-
> vives; and would end were that line to be extinguished; the
> extinction of all beings would make room for the new cast-
> ings Nature desires; to this end the one means is total de-
> struction, and that is the result toward which crime strives.
> Whence it comes out certainly that the criminal who could

> smite down the three kingdoms all at once by annihilating
> both them and their capacity to reproduce would be he who
> serves Nature best. (*J,* 770–71)

A too-perfect harmony would have still more drawbacks than disorder; if war, discord, and crimes were to be banished from the earth,
the spirit of the three kingdoms, having become too violent, would
then destroy all the other laws of Nature.

> Celestial bodies would come all to a halt, their influences
> would be suspended because of the overly great empire of
> one of their number; gravitation would be no more, and
> motion none. It is then the crimes of man which, stemming
> the rise of the kingdoms, counteracting their tendency to
> preponderate, prevent their importance from becoming
> such as must disrupt all else, and maintain in universal af-
> fairs that perfect equilibrium Horace called *rerum concordia
> discors.* Therefor is crime necessary in the world. But the
> most useful crimes are without doubt those which most dis-
> rupt, such as *refusal to propagate* and *destruction* . . . and thus
> you see these crimes . . . essential to the laws of Nature.
> [Yet] never will too many or enough murders be committed
> on earth, considering the burning thirst Nature has for
> them. (*J,* 771–72)

Sade rises here to the level of myth. The philosophy of his
century no longer suffices when it has to resolve the problem raised
by cruelty. As we have just seen, he would like to *integrate* cruelty
into a universal system in which, by recovering its cosmic function,
it would figure as pure cruelty. Consequently, the passions—from
the simple to the complex—have a transcendental import: though
man thinks he is satisfying himself by obeying them, in reality he is
satisfying only an aspiration that goes beyond his individual self.

> This murderer thinks he destroys, he thinks he consumes,
> and these beliefs sometimes engender remorse in his heart;
> let us put him confidently at ease, and if the system I have

just developed is a little beyond his reach, let us prove to
him from what happens before his very eyes that he has not
even the honor of destroying; that the annihilation upon
which he flatters himself when in sound health, or at which
he shudders when he is sick, is no annihilation at all, and
that annihilation is unfortunately something he cannot pos-
sibly achieve. (*J*, 769)[11]

Let us for a moment compare the principle of life and death
that will determine Sade's new position on the problem of destruction with the notion of the death instinct in Freud, who, in opposing this instinct to Eros, the instinct for life—for organic life—
established his ontological theory on these two notions. While
Freud envisions life only in the organic state, Sade—who despite
appearances is more of a metaphysican—does not admit a difference between life in the organic and in the inorganic state and does
not take into account considerations concerning the species, that
is, in the end, concerning the social milieu; there is in his conception but one principle:

In all living beings the principle of life is no other than that
of death: at the same time we receive the one we receive the
other, we nourish both within us, side by side. At the instant
we call *death*, everything seems to dissolve; we are led to
think so by the excessive change that appears to have been
brought about in this portion of matter which no longer
seems animate. But this death is only imaginary, it exists fig-
uratively but in no other way. Matter, deprived of the other
portion of matter which communicated movement to it, is
not destroyed for that; it merely abandons its form, it de-
cays—and in decaying proves that it is not inert; it enriches
the soil, fertilizes it, and serves in the regeneration of the
other kingdoms as well as of its own. There is, in the final
analysis, no essential difference between this first life we receive and this second, which is the one we call death. For
the first is caused by a forming of some of the matter which
renews and reorganizes itself within the entrails of mother
earth. . . . The first generation, which we call life, is as it

were an example. Only from exhaustion do its laws become operative; only through destruction are these laws transmitted; the former requires a kind of corrupted matter, the latter, petrified matter. And there is the sole cause of this immensity of successive creations: each of them consists of a repetition of the first principles of exhaustion or of destruction. (*J*, 769–70)

Corruption, putrefaction, dissolution, exhaustion, and annihilation—these aspects of the phenomena of life will have for Sade a meaning that is as much moral as physical. Only motion is real: creatures are but its changing phases. One is tempted to compare, no doubt with many reservations, this conception of perpetual motion with the Hindu doctrine of samsara. Would not Nature's aspiration to escape herself and return to the unconditioned state be a dream much like that of Nirvana—to the extent that a Western dreamer might be capable of such dreams? But instead of entering the path Schopenhauer searched for, Sade opens up one that Nietzsche will arrive at: the acceptance of samsara, of the eternal return of the Same.

4

Once the Sadean mind has acquired the notion of a Nature no longer wily like the Being Supreme in Wickedness, no longer voracious like the Minotaur, but a Nature who is the first slave of her own laws, the first of the victims of this universe, will not this mind consider itself a microcosm of this Nature, suffering, like Nature, of its own motion? This motion, instead of allowing Nature to bring about her complete realization, allows her only to create, to destroy, and to create anew with her creatures proofs of her own impotence. The Pope's *System* showed us two forces in competition: the aspiration in Nature to find again her most active power, and the principle of life and death of the three kingdoms, a principle of perpetual motion bringing about successive creations. But these forces are in fact but the same phenomenon: perpetual motion is blind, but the aspiration to escape the laws of this motion by destructions and crimes is but this motion become aware of itself. The Sadean mind will discover in this dualism its own inner conflict and will perhaps catch sight of its final solution. Is not Nature's problem with the creation-destruction of creatures also the problem of the reality of the other the Sadean mind has to deal with? Just as Nature creates obstacles by her own creative will, does not the Sadean mind create the neighbor in its will to create itself—which involves the necessity of destroying the other? It aspired to break this necessity; but through this aspiration toward innocence it admitted the existence of the other, it gave reality to the other, and thus remained in the necessity of destroying. And as it wished to maintain the other, it became guilty as soon as it maintained the other only so as to destroy him. Nature always aspires to and at the same time renounces her most active power; will then the Sadean mind be able to renounce the other and at the same time resolve on destruction?

5

If comparison with the wretched, indispensable for the libertine mind if it is to feel itself happy, presupposes the existence of the neighbor, the first step to take in the direction of a renaturalization of cruelty will be to deny the reality of the neighbor, to empty the notion of the neighbor of its content. In implying the neighbor's reality, the pleasure of comparison implied evil; the libertine mind would commit the error of converting the love of the neighbor, that "chimera" which haunted Sade, into a love-hatred of the neighbor. The love-hatred of the neighbor could only be a step on the path toward a liquidation of the reality both of the other and of oneself.

How could the Sadean mind ever renounce its object, the other, so as to resolve upon destroying purely and simply—in conformity with its representation of a Nature freed from the need to create? It will do so by renouncing not only the other but also its own individual condition as an ego.

In apparently solipsistic terms, many declarations of Sade's characters imply a doctrine with quite opposite conclusions. Under that entity which is *Nature aspiring to her most active power,* this doctrine posits absolute and sovereign desire as its principle. But in the name of this principle, it establishes between the self and the other a negative reciprocity:

> The false ideas which we have of the creatures who sur-
> round us are still the source of an infinite number of judg-
> ments whose moral basis is erroneous. We forge chimerical
> duties for ourselves where our relations with these creatures
> are concerned, simply because they think they have similar
> duties toward us. If we have the strength to renounce all
> that we expect from others, our duties toward them will be
> immediately annihilated. What, after all, are all the earth's
> creatures when measured against a single one of our
> desires? And by what right should I deprive myself of the
> least of my desires in order to please a creature who is noth-
> ing to me and who holds no interest whatsoever for me?[12]

But if the other is *nothing* for me, henceforth I am not only *nothing* for him but also *nothing* before my own consciousness— and in fact that consciousness is no longer still *mine.* For if I break with the other on the level of morality, I will have broken with my own self-possession on the level of existence itself. At any moment I can fall to the mercy of an other who will make the same declaration: "Let us have the strength to renounce . . . " The wager here is a pragmatic one. But Sade's reflection that prepares the way for this kind of declaration goes much further in its investigations.

The moral nihilism that tends to suppress consciousness of a self and consciousness of the other on the level of acts implies contradictions in Sade's reflection. This moral nihilism appears as the final consequence of atheism. For Sade could not limit himself to denying the existence of a personal God, who functioned as the principle of the responsible ego, the guarantor of the possession and the secrecy of such an ego; Sade also attacks this ego. As we have seen, he attacks the preservation and propagation of the species; he must now also put into question the normative principle of individuation, in order to give free rein to the forces of dissolution he described, the perversions, the anomalies—the emergence in the individual of sensuous polymorphy, at whose expense conscious individuation is accomplished in beings. Sade was not content with describing those forces of dissolution; he gave them the eloquence of the characters he created. These characters refute the existence of a God, guarantor of norms, but then plead in the language of these same norms the cause of the anomalies they represent. The anomalies are anomalies only inasmuch as they are expressed in this language, the language of consciousness. The language of consciousness can account for their positive content, the sensuous polymorphy, only in a negative way, in the negative formulations of the rational terminology Sade depends on. Here we are touching on the question of Sade's singular relationship with reason, where anomaly and thought constantly interact, where reason that wills to be universal is in contradiction with the most extreme form of reason reduced to itself which pleads for the particular case of anomaly. And at the same time we see the adventure consciousness undergoes; we see its misunderstandings and the traps it falls into, as soon as, reflecting the forces hostile to individuation, consciousness formulates them in an inverted form, in a discourse that requires a bearer.

Sade elucidates this misunderstanding without untangling it in an explicit way, but he has masked the trap involved here with his characters. For the trap in which we see the Sadean mind caught is also what makes it turn.

The dose of cruelty with which Nature has variously supplied

each individual is then taken to be only the frustrated impulse of
the desire with which each identifies himself in primary egocen-
trism, as though he were its sole bearer. But in fact this impulse
would tend to the destruction of that individual as much as it tends
to the destruction of others.

He who asks, What, after all, are all the earth's creatures
when measured against a single one of our desires? is already a
victim of misunderstanding, a plaything of an impulse that questions itself, that is individuated but that resents its individuation.
The impulse of desire can give its own absolute character to the
individual, who in return speaks for the desire that has no language. The question that the individual formulates gets its violence
from the impulse caught in the individual, who is suffering from
that violence as much as he would like to make the other suffer.
Thus he turns against the others the challenge he addresses to himself: Let us have the strength to renounce all that we expect from
others. . . . A formula for a break with others that compensates for
its rhetorical solipsism by putting back into question the consciousness of itself.

With this move, we see Sade, whose concept of a Nature destructive of her own works had identified destruction with the purity of desire, now set out to find an outlet for the necessity to
destroy in a negation of destruction. This is the project of his morality of apathy; its therapeutics must bring about this renunciation
of the reality of self.

The practice of apathy, such as the characters Sade created
recommend, presupposes that what are called *soul, conscience, sensitivity, heart*, are but the diverse structures that the concentration of
the same impulsive forces take on. Under pressure from the world
of others, these forces can elaborate the structure of an instrument
of intimidation; when these forces are internal, they can elaborate
the structure of an instrument of subversion—and they always do
so instantaneously. In fact the impulses that intimidate us make
insurgents of us at the same time, and the impulses are ever the
same.

Blot out your soul—try to find pleasure in everything that
alarms your heart; arrive quickly . . . at the perfection of
this brand of stoicism; in apathy you will discover a whole
host of new pleasures which are delectable in a way quite
different from those you think are found in the source of
your fatal sensitivity. Don't you think that in my childhood I
had a heart like you? But I restrained this organ, and in this
voluptuous harshness I discovered the source of multiple
deviations and pleasures that are of more import than my
weaknesses. . . . On the basis of my errors I have established principles; since that time, I have known felicity.

How does this intimidating insurrection or this insurrectional
intimidation act in us? Through images, which form prior to acts
and incite us to act or to suffer acts, and through images of acts
committed which return to us and torment conscience with remorse as much as the idle impulses restore it. But "on the one
hand, the impossibility of reparation, on the other, that of making
out which of your crimes you ought to repent most, and the conscience, first dizzied, then rendered incoherent, is finally reduced
to utter silence; thus we see that conscience is distinct from all
other maladies of the soul, it dwindles away to nothingness as more
is added to it" (J, 641).

Elsewhere Sade observes that the same is true of sensitivity:
"To extend it is to annihilate it."[13] This confirms his belief that the
same impulses are at work in both the structures of the organ of
intimidation and that of the organ of subversion. Thus the consciousness of ourselves and of others is the most fragile and the
most transparent of functions. Then, as soon as our impulses intimidate us by creating fear or remorse through the images of actions to be undertaken or of actions committed, we must substitute
acts, of whatever kind, for images of acts each time the images
would tend to substitute themselves for or get in the way of acts.
Thus Juliette is encouraged to do

immediately, in cold blood, that very thing which, done in
the throes of passion, has been able to cause you remorse

when later on you recover your wits. This way you strike
squarely and hard at the virtuous impulse the instant it
bares itself; and this custom of attacking it head on at the
first sign of its reappearance, and it tends to reappear once
the senses have subsided into calm, this, I say, is one of the
most certain fashions of destroying it definitively; employ
this secret, it never fails: directly a moment of calm favors
the resurgence of vice, announcing itself under the colors
of remorse, for that is always the guise it wears in its en-
deavor to regain ascendancy over us—then, directly when
you perceive it, commit forthwith the act you are wont to
regret. . . . (*J*, 450)

How can this practice of apathy become a viable method for
the achievement of "voluptuous hardness"? For what, in fact,
could be more self-contradictory than the break with the other
Sade enjoins? For him, the abolition of our duties to others and the
exclusion of others from one's sensibility would always be translated into acts which, in order to be violent, require the other. The
acts, then, reestablish the reality of the other and of myself.

If the other is now nothing for me, and I nothing for the
other, how could these acts, issuing from a nothing and directed
upon another nothing, be brought about?

If this nothing is never again to be filled by the reality of the
other and the reality of myself, filled neither by enjoyment nor by
remorse, it is necessary that I disappear in an endless reiteration of
acts—which I run the risk of regretting, because as soon as they are
suspended the reality of the other imposes itself on me once again.
Or I run the risk of overestimating the enjoyment those acts procure me as soon as I relate this enjoyment or this regret to myself,
or relate them to the other as to their source.

What then would be the error of Saint-Fond—that perfect
figure of the perverse libertine who has not gone beyond the stage
of negative sympathy? That of conceding to his victim as much reality as to himself. What happened is that his consciousness was in-
timidated by its own impulses, such that he wants to hurl himself on

his victim—always the same victim—throughout eternity. His self-consciousness remains a function of the representation that he continually forms of the self-consciousness his victim has when he suffers, which self-consciousness makes that victim an accomplice in the delights of his torturer.

The morality of apathy dictates that such acts be reiterated—to what aim? Sade has grasped the difficulty well, even though he may not have resolved the dilemma: the enjoyment negative contact with the other still procures me must be prevented as much as remorse. For here remorse is but the other side of enjoyment; they form two different behaviors out of the same impulses. Henceforth acts must be informed, not by the enjoyment that the quality peculiar to one victim would procure, but solely by the negation of objects that provokes such acts. Then, for the reiteration of acts to be able to have the significance of a negation of destruction itself—emptying destruction of all content—number, the quantity of the objects sacrificed, becomes the object of these acts. With quantity the objects are depreciated; the reality both of the other and of the self are dissolved. Thus the morality of apathy, which commands the greatest impulsive agitation, wishes to make this agitation coincide with a no less extreme vigilance to ensure the purity of those impulses. And if the practice of this morality consists in doing immediately in cold blood the same thing that, done in frenzy, was able to give us remorse, such a rule could serve virtue as well as vice, whenever a virtuous impulse might cause us some remorse. "Virtue itself will safeguard you from remorse, for you shall have acquired the habit of doing evil at the first virtuous prompting; and to cease doing evil you shall have to stifle virtue" (*J*, 450).

Could this be the solution to the dialectical drama of the Sadean mind—if, that is, this mind, by its very definition, does not exclude every solution? To get beyond the notion of evil, which is conditioned by the degree of reality accorded the other, we have seen this mind exalt the ego to the limit. But the culmination of this exaltation was to be in the apathy in which, when the other is abolished, the ego is abolished at the same time, in which enjoyment is dissociated from destruction, and in which destruction is identified with desire in its pure form. In this way the Sadean mind reproduces in its reflection the perpetual motion of a Nature who creates but arouses obstacles for herself with those very creations and, for a moment, finds her freedom only in destroying her own works.

Under
the Mask of
Atheism

1. Destruction and Purity

Let us now turn again to Sade himself. We have only constructed a system with the statements and practices of his characters, which he himself used to make intelligible the unrelenting course of the life he lived. The terms *Nature* and *perpetual motion* have served only to transfer the mystery and incomprehensibility of God into metaphysical entities, without resolving or exhausting that mystery of being which is the possibility of evil and of nothingness. In this development of representations, elaborated in the terminology of the period, let us now restrict our attention to the pathos that is continuously expressed in it. A pathos of the soul enchained, which rattles its chains and sees in the universe it inhabits only a creation likewise in chains, a creation made in the image of a creative Nature that is unable to realize itself once and for all. A pathos of imprisonment and impotence, of the impatience of being a creature. For it is indeed being that is experienced here as the ultimate prison, the outermost wall; and duration in the unendurable length and emptiness of time is an experience of being chained to one's condition. Beyond the wall, there is the freedom of nonbeing, the freedom of God, who is accused of incarcerating his creatures in the prison of being.

In the soul of this libertine great lord of the century of the Enlightenment, very old mental structures are reawakened; it is impossible not to recognize the whole ancient system of the Manichaean gnosis, the visions of Basilides, Valentinus, and especially Marcion. Such a conception once again has its source in the sentiment of a fall of the spirit and the obscure memory of original purity. The present state attests to a fall, and the present age can be filled only with waiting, in the absence of any redemption—only with the sentiment of an unceasing fall, of a progressive degradation. Such a conception, contrary to every idea of progress, radically opposes Sade to his whole century; it sets him up against Rousseau, Voltaire, and Robespierre and brings him singularly close to Saint-Just, and even more to Joseph de Maistre and Baudelaire.

The act of creation is itself a consequence of the fall; creating is the act of revolt of a demiurge against the pure God of the spirits. The whole of creation then bears the seal of a curse; the human body, like every physical organism, is the image not of a divine creator but of the imprisonment of the spirits. All these themes are easily found again in Sade's thoughts. If this sentiment of a fall and of a curse makes Sade's thought akin to that of Maistre, this sentiment is, however, too obscurely experienced, within the order of rationalist terminology, to recognize itself expressed in the dogma of original sin, which Maistre will reaffirm. This sentiment resorts to myth—*which is only the form the oblivion of a revealed truth takes.*

We thus understand why Sade's clandestine work shows much more natural affinity with the great heresiarchs of Gnosticism. The erotic scenes themselves are distinguishable from the current literary genre of his age by the hatred of the body, by the impatience provoked in his heroes by the patient men and women they torment, and by the frenzied cult of orgasm, which was in certain Manichaean sects a form of the cult of *original light.*

In Sade's public work, in particular in *Crimes of Love,* the leitmotiv is, like in his clandestine works, that of a myth of an original purity become inaccessible; whence the obsession with virginity, the basic experience of Sade's temperament.

This myth arose from the constraint put on Sade's genius and temperament by the terminological discipline of his time. The positivist reference to the phenomena of Nature leads Sade to put himself in Nature; this is why there is in Sade's work really a spectacle of Nature, which he looks upon as though it were the spectacle of his own mind. He is thus secretly close not only to the Gnostics of Christian antiquity but also to those German Gnostics, the *Naturphilosophen,* especially Schelling and Hegel, for whom Nature is but a dramatic procession of Mind. In telling us of an original Nature and of the rival natures that deprive her of her power, Sade constructs less a cosmology than a pneumatology translated into the terms of the materialist philosophy of the age, a Gnostic theory of the fall of the spirits. The Germans have continued to cultivate such a theory in a more traditional form because of their more vivid sense of the phenomenon of the numinous. Sade presents us with the fiction of an original Nature that raises up before herself rival natures (the three kingdoms, the human species) in that perpetual motion which seeks to fulfill original Nature once and for all but instead only continues to create and destroy and therefore never escapes its imprisonment in creatures. How could we not recognize in this account the fall of a pure spirit, either the pure God of the spirits or one of those spirits that had revolted against God and been condemned to the impotence of perpetual motion? The Being Supreme in Wickedness described by Saint-Fond (the Prime Minister in *Juliette*) has all the features of Marcion's demiurge, that is, of the creative God of Moses. In the eyes of this heresiarch, the creative God of Moses, because he is a God of law and justice, was the adversary of a God who was foreign to this world created for suffering. It is this alien God, a true God of Love, who had, motivated by pure goodness, sent forth his Son as light into this, the demiurge's world. Original Nature, as the Pope expounds it to Juliette in his *System,* appears, in comparison with the God of

Saint-Fond, as an intermediary divinity between the wicked and justice-dealing God of Marcion and a fallen spirit, such as Origen's Lucifer, who still obscurely recalls the splendor enjoyed in the purity of his first condition, before his revolt against the God of the spirits. Because of this obscure memory of lost purity that remains in the fallen spirit, Origen, a father of the Eastern church, explicitly admitted that the Redemption of Christ includes all the created worlds, that of the spirits as well as that of men, and would also extend to the hell of Satan himself, who at the end of time would be the last one saved and redeemed in his turn.

In this system of an original Nature and rival natures, the hidden goal of perpetual motion is then not motion itself but the original purity of the spirits. The agency of this aspiration of Nature to definitive fulfillment is destruction, which is seen to be intimately associated with the idea of purity. Here we find the basis of the Sadean idea of pure crime.

Sade's system is like a strange synthesis of the antagonist gods of Marcion: Sade's Nature appears to recall the state of purity of Marcion's alien god, but in order to reach that state of purity, this Nature, because it has fallen into the snare its own creation is for it, has to resort to the cruel God of justice whom Marcion identified with the God of Revelation. We then find ourselves witnessing the struggle of a spirit that, instead of manifesting in creation its virtual riches and in history its supreme intentions, like Mind in Hegel, becomes, on contact with its creatures, conscious of them as its errors. Then, far from acting to save them, it uses them for its own redemption, its own deliverance. The economy of salvation is inverted; human sufferings redeem a fallen spirit by enabling it to purify itself.

2.   Homage to the Virgin

The myth that associated purity with destruction is of interest only because it clarifies the Sadean mind itself. For in this myth this mind only describes how it arrives at knowing itself so as to enjoy its own organization.

Purity is an absolute quality which the Sadean mind has dissociated from the creative God. Since creation is an occasion of fall, it is necessary to abolish the Creator and destroy creation. But he who wishes to destroy for the sake of purity is himself a creature who participates in being; his first natural movement is to attach himself to the beloved object in order to preserve it. In the eyes of him who has conceived of purity apart from the creative God, destruction and purity are confused and become a single absolute demand that he can no more evade than he can shield from it the beloved object to which he is naturally disposed to attach himself. What the adept of purity does is attach himself to the object and preserve it only in order to destroy it; the demand for purity makes him impure and cruel. We always find the same opposing themes: Creation is an occasion of fall and will then be interpreted as a sign of fall. This sign must be abolished; yet the need to preserve this creation must be affirmed, for it is what enables one to bring about destruction.

A creature is an occasion of a fall—but which creature does Sade have in mind? The virgin is an image of divine purity; at the same time she is a sign of the fall of him who desires her simply as a creature. As an image of the purity of God, the virgin is excluded from possession by man; but man cannot forget that she is possessable. She becomes in Sade a motif of exasperation, and prohibition, of virility.

The image of the virgin, because of the reaction it provokes in Sade, is already an image of his own cruelty—which it announces and provokes. We find ourselves here before something that corresponds to the religious ascesis expressed in courtly love.[1] In courtly love, the image of virginal purity exalts virility over and beyond the instinct for procreation and associates it with the love of God. The image of the virgin, an incarnation of celestial purity, at first an adorable object in itself, becomes a mediator for adoration purified of all carnal passion. But in the Sadean experience the image of the virgin, perceived as a paradoxical creature, exasperates virility and, instead of exalting it over and beyond the instinct for procreation, turns it against this instinct; the effect of this image is to associate virility intimately with the practice of cruelty. The paradoxical image of the virgin, a sign prohibiting virile possession, has for Sade the value of assimilating celestial purity with destruction and the unpossessable virginal flesh with a curse on virility. The accursed virility is experienced only as the motive for the loss of its object, and it finds in the curse upon it a compensatory taste of bitterness, of which the virgin, source of its cruelty, is the designated object. Then the image of celestial purity incarnate will become for Sade's soul the indispensable pretext for his aspiration to destroy incorporeal purity. A secret complicity forms between this image, an object of possession qua creature but excluding possession qua sign, and the virility accursed by this image. The virginal image, image of something subject to abuse because it is adorable, will inspire in Sade the worst offense that accursed virility could inflict on its object. Sade's soul thereby not only compensates for its initial defeat but affirms the compensation for it.

Such is the experience at the basis of Sade's temperament and of his most profound literary creation, the story of Justine, the story of a virgin subjected to the rigors of the resentment of exasperated virility. This tale recounts the trial that virginity is made to undergo not only because it incarnates the purity of God but also because it represents what is at stake in this purity: the immortality of the soul and blessed eternity, fruit of and compensation for the sufferings of this life, including the suffering of the exasperated virility of Sade himself. But Sade no longer wants any compensations except those that the exasperation of virility has given him: the full exercise of cruelty.

The proceedings he draws up against the virgin, against the religious idea of virginity, are hardly surprising in a materialist and anti-Christian epoch; virginity appears in this period as a state as absurd from the point of view of the unbeliever as the idea of conjugal fidelity. Yet Sade's soul nonetheless obscurely aspires to purity and fidelity as to goals that have become incomprehensible.

For Sade, purity can only be disembodied and can result only from destruction, and fidelity can consist only in an indefatigable assault on the same victim. Thus cruelty for him is a fidelity, and an homage to the virgin and to God, an homage become incomprehensible to itself.

Indeed, all of Sade's work has appeared to us as one desperate cry, hurled at the image of inaccessible virginity, a cry enveloped and as it were enshrined in a canticle of blasphemies: I am excluded from purity because I wish to possess the one who is pure. I cannot not desire purity, but at the same time I am impure because I wish to enjoy purity, which excludes enjoyment.

The word *virtue* in Sade has no other meaning but that of virginal purity. This purity has to be constantly besmirched in order to make it constantly present. Such is the underlying theme in the tale of the pair of sisters Justine and Juliette.

Justine, a virtuous girl, will be tirelessly thrown into the worst and most humiliating situations contrived to tear her secret from her. In the end Sade will have to call upon nothing less than a bolt of lightning to suppress her. This lightning is the image both of purity and of wrath, the image of the wrath of God and of the wrath of those damned to the hell of impurity. Sade elevates and definitively consecrates the virgin by this holocaust.

Juliette, the vicious girl, can only redouble her energies devoted to vice to compensate for the ardor of Justine's purity. In Sade's eyes, she is a Justine whose secret has been torn from her but who has remained in fact ungraspable. One crime, or two, or a hundred are not enough to reveal this secret; she must be pushed into ever greater crimes, crimes commensurate with the infinite purity of her sister, Justine. In narrating her adventures, which have no reason ever to come to an end, Sade wishes to forget the vexation that the loss of the unpossessable Justine causes him.

Everything in Sade will thus predispose him, in these last years of the century of Voltaire, to speak the language of a latent Jansenism. Corrupt nature and human love undergo the consequences of a damnation, and faith now in decline no longer delivers them from the eternal punishments they have themselves pronounced on themselves. But this inconsolable vexation will in the end take the place of faith. Before it becomes that value which will be most characteristically illustrated in the work of Sénancour, this vexation has become the focal point of Sade's soul, though it escapes his view, blinded by rationalism. The terminology the author of *Justine* uses offers him only notions emptied of their content by an age that thought it saw in self-interest the motive force of human acts. This narrowness, this poverty of conventional psychology, forced the monster-author to imagine improbable situations[2] in order to describe the reality he was experiencing. What is terrible in virginal purity is that it hides from me that by which it perhaps is escaping me. Is suspicion of its purity then the most certain means to ensure possession of, not a particular woman, but the secret of purity?

Some of the tales of *Crimes of Love* seek to translate the different aspects of this fundamental theme into the terms of conventional norms. "Florville," "Eugénie de Franval," "Ernestine," and "Miss Henriette Stralson" are cases in point.

Florville presents herself to her future spouse as an honorable and sincere young woman who intends to enlighten him about her strange past. In this tale, there is no suspicion in the man; M. de Courval not only does not seem jealous of those who have accidentally preceded him in the arms of his future spouse but seems to be sunk into a sort of unconsciousness from which he will only gradually awaken. This unconsciousness is significant. He sought happiness in conjugal life, but in fact he sought oblivion, for he too is guilty. This is the true motive for his sympathy for Florville. When

Florville has finished her confession, everything seems to work out: Courval, who was first described to us as a man who desires to savor only the honorable pleasure of conjugal life, wishes to conclude his marriage with all haste precisely because, it seems, of the lubricious adventures of his future spouse. It is clear that under the cover of an exceptional generosity, Courval incarnates the Sadean satisfaction of possessing Florville's apparently revealed secret. But in fact the Sadean suspicion is incarnated in the heroine herself; Florville is an enigma to herself, as is the human soul at the beginning of its journey, before being able to know itself as God alone knows it. The author's own demon has lodged itself in Florville; it will possess her until it reveals her to herself as she is. "Why did it have to be that the unhappy Florville, the most virtuous, most lovable, and most sensitive of beings, finds herself, because of an unseemly evolution of fate, the most abominable monster that nature could create?"

Brought up in a convent where she spent her girlhood years, Florville, faced with the gravity and the accumulation of her misdeeds, puts an end to her life. This is not the denouement of a plot; it is the solution of an enigma. The turns of fortune have revealed a soul that was guilty before it had acted. Sade's heroes are sleepwalkers in broad daylight. The stupefaction of a soul when faced with itself is the true theme of this tale.

"Eugénie de Franval" takes up again the theme of jealousy and suspicion, this time in its most frightful form, that over paternal incest consciously committed as an act of defiance of divine and human laws. The character of Franval and that of his wife have certain autobiographical elements. Mme. de Franval has all the characteristics of the Marquise, all the virtues of love, devotion, and resignation she displayed before the recidivist character of the Marquis. And Franval, more than any other of Sade's characters, shows all of Sade's uncontrollable drive, along with that cunning that masks, with the jealousy and suspicion of a demanding husband, a deeper jealousy and suspicion. Here again, Franval is but an image of the obsession for a purity craved and inaccessible, and paternal incest is the immediate means used to take possession of virginity. Virginity can be possessed only in woe, since its possession entails its corruption and hence its loss. If Franval runs up against no obstacle or barrier in himself before the consummation of incest, he nonetheless sets up barriers outside. His inner freedom cannot be exercised without crime and costs him his social freedom. The way a first transgression is ramified in transgressions it irremediably engenders is here described with the customary vigor of the Marquis: from incest to adultery, from adultery to false witness, from false witness to murder. In vain the priest—who in this tale plays the role not so much of religion as of the morality of common sense—seeks to demonstrate this to the sophisticated Franval. Franval defends his situation with a fanaticism, even a fervor that, however far they have gone in sin, and perhaps because they have gone so far, bring him ever closer to God, whose wrath he provokes—closer than does the deist and social morality of the ecclesiastic, wholly marked with the humanitarian incredulity of his century. Here we touch on mystery in Sade. Incest, like every other perversion, appears irreducible to human reason, with the irreducibility to human reason characteristic of sin. Reason can do nothing to right fallen nature, because reason deprived of faith remains the plaything of this nature. The refusal to kneel before a moral and nonetheless strictly human authority is in Franval only a provocation addressed to God, absent from the spirit of the age.

Why do these tales, which pretend to be moral, appear to us to be so ambiguous? Because the rational morality that serves as a criterion for the teller presupposes a human consciousness and freedom exceeded at every moment by the dark forces at work. These forces tend to a light and also into a darkness that the rational morality of self-interest and conscience reduced to social proportions can only be unaware of. This light and this darkness are known only in the revealed order; these dark forces require, not a Supreme Being, but the reference to a personal God who alone knows them, whose curse they have suffered to the point of having forgotten this God. In those whom these forces move and over-whelm, after having forgotten their judge, there remains now only the movement unto darkness that ends in the oblivion of their own existence. The world Sade describes for us is that of fault which comes to be unaware of itself once more. Though the Decalogue has become obscure and lifeless, fault has become again a form of affectivity, an evil that sought in vain to extinguish itself in the death of Sade's characters, an evil that will survive them in the reveries of Obermann, will obsess Adolphe, will make Maldoror delirious.

In *The Story of Justine and Juliette,* Sade writes as though he had nothing more pressing in view than to discredit atheism; liber-tinage and crimes are the immediate application of the theoretical negation of the immortality of the soul. To reduce their victims to the state of human rags, to arouse the reflexes of animal nature in the human being—these are first the rational goal of Sade's char-acters. But the demonstration given is a clumsy one; the reiteration of tortures and the continuous efforts expended on one sole victim (they go on to another victim only reluctantly, because they are aware of not having attained their goal) prove to the contrary that the insatiability of their soul is commensurate with its immortality. This is so much the case that their operations seem to make a con-trary demonstration: the soul destroys the body because it does not succeed in destroying itself. And perhaps an obscure, wholly Mani-chaean hatred of creation presides over their orgies. The charac-ters in *Justine and Juliette* spend their time killing the soul; at the end of the ten volumes of the novel we have to conclude they have not succeeded. What then is the meaning of the suicides of the characters in *Crimes of Love?* Franval cannot resist the "violent agi-tation of remorse" to which his daughter has already succumbed. Florville wishes to escape her own monstrousness. They all hope to find rest in the "eternal sleep" which the powers of their souls and divine and human laws have refused them. There would be much to say about this need for rest in Sade's creatures. Here let us only take note of their act; it seems to us to be something else than an expedient means to conclude a tale. If we are to believe what they say, these suicides are punitive and liberating; but what they say is still fiction, as is the conscience that inspires them. In fact the soul has not succeeded in inflicting death on itself; it then resorts to that simulacrum of the death of the soul which is suicide. "Cum ergo quisque credens, quod post mortem non erit, intolerabilibus tamen molestiis ad totam cupiditatem mortis impellitur, et decernit atque arripit mortem, in opinione habet errorem omnimodae defectionis, in sensu autem naturale desiderium quietis. *Quod autem quietum est, non est nihil: immo etiam magis est, quam id quod inquietum est*" (St. Augustine, *De libero arbitrio*).

Additional Note concerning Justine

Sade has entrusted the playing out of his ideas to two feminine figures who will pay what those ideas cost, each in her own way, the one in suffering from them, the other in trying them out. Sade seems to have put all of himself in the two sisters Justine and Juliette, in preference to masculine characters. To recount the parallel lives of two women equally beautiful but of different temperaments, thrown into analogous situations but reacting in accordance with opposite principles, was no doubt to invest his tale with considerable moral interest, and the project certainly offered advantages for his demonstrations. In addition, it is clear that, by identifying himself with these two feminine characters, experiencing emotions as women can experience them, the creator of Justine and Juliette drew from his own inner depths to create the substance of these two figures as much as he drew from his experiences. In the character of Justine it could be that Sade experienced the torments and bitterness of his own mind, the humiliations and vexations he suffered because of his frankness. In the ingenuousness of her sensibility Justine personifies Christian morality; her fate could indeed, mutatis mutandis, represent the fate of the author, who carried out in practice all the moral consequences of his profession of atheism and saw himself exposed to all the persecutions a society apparently Christian was capable of. This is the society to which Justine, who thinks she is obeying its rules honestly, is subjected. But neither Christian society nor a "normal" human nature exists. Justine, in her fidelity to the illusion that they do, becomes the pretext and the point of departure for the development of all turpitudes, perversions, crimes, that is, all "anomalies." Even more, because of her illusion about herself, her purity, wherever she turns up Justine provokes evil in the different characters she encounters. Not only does the way she attracts men and women make her know new forms of perversity at the hands of others, but in addition the dilemmas that her purity brings into each new situation make her the accomplice of the crimes that are committed about her. Justine thus personifies all by herself the taboo indispensable for the Sadean enterprise. The action develops out of the existing state, the admitted norms, the institutions; these are to be overthrown within the feminine character who is their spokesperson, ceaselessly opposed, violently beset upon, always in tears. In showing Justine always true to herself from the first rape to the worst defilements, Sade knows how to exploit all the more forcefully the horror and distress of a consciousness hunted down in its final refuge, where it sees itself attacked in its inviolable self-possession, in the representations the self has of its own integrity. For consciousness always remains inseparable from the body that is in its eyes lost but whose carnal reflexes threaten to betray its secret. This secret is that the ego is in danger of being alienated by itself and losing its identity. Justine thus experiences unhappy consciousness for not having admitted the absolute reality of evil in her own flesh and the perversity in her own nature; the worst of her humiliations is that she herself experiences the forbidden pleasures that her tormentors force upon her. And this is the goal of the experiment Sade conducts on the character of Justine. Here what is original with him is the way he describes her, making the reader follow the reverberations of each operation in the consciousness of the heroine, to the point that the reader sees Justine outside of herself, attacking the principles of her own conscience: "Always between vice and virtue, must the path of happiness never open for me save by delivering me over to infamies!"

The figure of Juliette, conceived much later than that of Justine, is also therefore more complex. In her illusions concerning norms and institutions Justine's perspective was that of a victim. Juliette's perspective is that of the torturers and monsters in whose hands institutions are exploited for the purposes of their own anomalies. (For what this character represents in Sade's work, see what we have said concerning the androgyne in our study "The Philosopher-Villain.")

3. *Delectatio Morosa*

For accursed virility, cruelty is the means of overcoming the experience of the loss of the beloved object. Accursed virility discharges its cruelty on the object that escapes it and finds in that cruelty an exaltation that has been refused it in love. Sade's characters thus acquire the habit of fictitiously losing by lingering over their victims: I wish that you unendingly cease to exist so that I could unendingly lose you, unendingly destroy you. Their behavior constitutes, then, the reverse of that of the characters created by romanticism, who through fear of becoming guilty of impurity before the beloved object and incurring the punishment that the loss of that object would be for them, implore that beloved object thus: I wish to suffer in order to eternally deserve to keep you. But the characters romanticism created have in common with those Sade created the experience of a deficiency in being and of time without eternity. If romantics like Jean-Paul, Jacobi, or Hölderlin hope to communicate with the eternal in the absolute nature of passion, which for them takes the place of the love of God, other romantics

like Chateaubriand, Sénancour, or Benjamin Constant are close
kin to Sade's characters, who experience the eternal only in the
mode of the ennui of their now-idle souls. Sade's characters find in
destructive time both the accomplice of and the expression of their
own inclination for destruction. But what makes them agree to this
inclination is the need to overcome the same experience of the loss
of the beloved object which haunted the characters depicted by
romanticism. Behind the creation of all these characters, we find
the conscious divorce with God and the loss of the sentiment of the
eternal which has not yet broken the affective unity of the soul.
Since one cannot alienate a soul made for eternity, the loss of the
sentiment of the eternal translates into an everlasting ennui of the
soul.

The notion of *delectatio morosa*[3] formulated by the doctors of
the medieval church singularly expresses this state characteristic of
the generations posterior to the ages of faith, as though those profound students of the human heart had already grasped the evil of
modern times, that which Revelation calls "the torment of the
scorpion's sting in a man." "In those days men sought death and
did not find it; they wanted to die and death fled far from them"
(Revelation 9:5–6). For in its ennui the soul seeks to inflict death on
itself; separated from god, its immortality has turned into bitterness.

The suffering of the soul subjected to all the length of time
undergone in ennui, in which the soul feels all the weight of its own
immortality become alien to itself; the enjoyment the soul finds in
its own delirium, which liberates it from ennui—this is what *delectatio morosa* designates. It is the habitual activity of Sade's soul, con-
tracted in the course of long years of confinement in state prisons.

Morose delectation consists in that movement of the soul by
which it bears itself voluntarily toward images of forbidden carnal
or spiritual acts in order to linger in contemplation of them. These
images of temptation or of sin already committed belong to spontaneous revery, and their appearance does not of itself constitute a

sinful state from the point of view of moral theology, no more than does the temptation to sin constitute sin itself. But when the soul sets out to fix these images whenever they present themselves to chance revery or, with a presentiment of their hidden presence, to evoke them when they have apparently vanished into the dark zone of the mind as means of pleasure that the soul would have in reserve in its caverns, it is then and only then that, through the intervention of the will, the soul gives itself over to a necessarily guilty occupation. Such is the essentially juridical point of view of moral theology, whose role is to determine the moment in which the sin of morose delectation becomes flagrant. But this determination is purely casuist and has no other purpose than to forestall the scruples of a troubled conscience and to alert souls whose propensity for revery is excessive.

This notion of *delectatio morosa* is of interest inasmuch as it designates and describes this voluntary adhesion of the soul to the spontaneous movement of revery. But where does revery properly so-called stop and morose delectation begin? Is not revery already the symptom of a soul that has left its supernatural state, that seeks to elude its own vocation, and knows then the ennui that follows its uprootedness, its abandonment of God, and the alienation of the sentiment of eternity? Is not revery the spontaneous adhesion to the ruinous movement of time—when the soul, promised for the time of God, no longer adheres to the time of maturation in prayer?

It is useful for us to recall here the dispositions that introduce revery. Consciousness abandons itself to the slow work of dissolution by the dark forces, a dissolution that goes on in the dreams of sleeping consciousness. Revery allows one to intercept the first stages of this work of dissolution. Consciousness can make itself the accomplice of this dissolution in the deliberate way the consciousness of an ascetic subjects the powers of his soul to the practice of privation—in the course of which the initial intention, conceived in faith, survives the stages of the asceticism and finds in them its fulfillment. The Christian ascetic uses experienced time as a ladder to reach the eternity of the divine core of the soul, in which God is more inward to the soul than the soul is to itself. But the dreamer casts himself into time like the desperate man who, not having been able to decide on suicide, resolves at least to cast himself into the swirling ocean, leaving to the element its freedom to swallow him up, but allowing for the chance that he will come out safe and sound if he finds strength again in his arms. In such a state Sade's consciousness watches its progressive invasion by the powers of the soul along with all the objects that have affected them.

In Sade, *delectatio morosa* has thus become a creative function, constitutive of his consciousness. Not only does Sade dream; he directs his dream and leads it back to the object that is at the origin of his revery, as methodically as a skilled religious contemplative who puts his soul in a state of prayer before a divine mystery. The Christian soul becomes aware of itself before God; the romantic soul, which is now but a state nostalgic for faith, becomes conscious of itself in setting up its passion as an absolute, making the state of pathos its life function. The Sadean soul, for its part, becomes conscious of itself only through the object that exasperates its virility and constitutes its consciousness in that state of exasperated virility—which likewise becomes a paradoxical life function. This soul feels itself alive only in exasperation.

The Christian soul gives itself over to God; the romantic soul to its nostalgia; the Sadean soul to its exasperation. In giving itself over to God, the soul knows that God gives himself over to the soul. But nostalgia and exasperation can restore to the soul only the permanent state of nostalgia and exasperation.

Whereas in exterior reality the subject finds himself submitted to the spatial conditions of his search for, search after, and encounter with beings and things, in inward reality the contrary is the case: in the space of the soul, beings and things come to the subject and join with him through the sentiment the subject has of them in the expectation of their approach.

For the religious contemplative, for the ascetic, this interiorization of the visible world, this inward experience of things and beings in the space of the soul, will compete with the spiritual realities of the invisible world, the images of divine realities. All the exercises of the purgative way—the purification of the senses that actualize the absent things—consist in a relentless struggle with this threatening crowd of images of terrestrial goods and creatures to be transcended, a struggle to open the way of the soul toward its divine core.

For the one who gives himself over to diurnal revery and strives to retain its images, *delectatio morosa* presents itself exactly as an inverted spiritual exercise. For, materially speaking, it consists in cultivating the memory of the senses frustrated of their object, and in converting this memory into a faculty that evokes the absent things. In the end, the very absence of the objects becomes the condition sine qua non for this faculty of representation in the frustrated sensibility.

The Christian ascetic and the awake dreamer (which Sade is) know, then, an equivalent experience of lived time. Spontaneous revery brings back the past of their life and represents it either as a sin committed or else as a temptation. In solitude the present can at any time be filled by the representation of absent or past things. Against this the ascetic marshals prayer, meditation, invocation, which are not only states of pure and simple aspiration after God but efficacious actions that deprive the natural sensibility of its faculty to actualize absent things, so as to make it purely receptive of a presence that that faculty was turning it away from. There is more: this faculty that actualizes absent things is at work in the purely psychic space of the soul where move those dark forces that ascetic theology names the lower powers. The soul's reaction by prayer— its resistance to the spontaneous movement of revery, its emancipation with regard to its faculty that actualizes absent things for the benefit of a presence that is that of its own divine core—has, at the same time, opened to the soul the space of spiritual reality. It is only in this space that the soul knows itself as the locus of divine presence and experiences God as both the locus of its own origin and the supreme object of its deepest craving. By developing spiritual senses oriented toward the representation of holy realities, the ascetic abolishes the world of past things. Not only are they then ended for it, but they are not even absent; they have gone out of being because the newly developed senses have found another pasture. The appraisal of past life as a life sinful before God—before the God who is the inexhaustible source of affect for these new senses—gives the soul the strength it needs to free itself from the necessity of recommencing acts that would break with this affect. Such acts can no longer require their repetition and the projects for them can no longer require their realization, because the soul, having reached its divine core, no longer seeks to affirm itself in these acts; God, its sole affirmation, is also its freedom. But Sade's soul given over to revery is materially prevented by a constraint, perhaps as inward as it is exterior, from realizing what it dreams of, and it knows the time it experiences only as a duration intolerable to itself. It suffers from its being-in-potency as though it never stopped coming out of nothingness without ever arriving at being: I exist so as not to exist.

Unlike the believing soul, which is defined by the presence of God in it as an affirmation of itself, Sade's soul, concealing its fundamental exasperation under an atheist consciousness, is first defined as the negation of itself. This soul must forget its secret wound, which it can do only by alienating God, its Creator and Judge, for God, like the image of the virgin, is the painful recall of its accursed virility. It then turns away from the eternal, from its own divine core, and gives itself over wholly to revery, to a dreamy contemplation of the time that ruins beings and things, hoping for oblivion and for the destruction of the fundamental object of its memory. Thus the atheist consciousness, born from Sade's wounded soul, seeks to repudiate, along with the existence of God, its own immortality, while yielding to the chagrin in this repudiated soul. This consciousness suffocates remorse so as to obtain oblivion; it wishes to devalue purely and simply whatever the soul would have experienced before. In the movement of its revery it will imagine itself to be a free being by recommencing the outline of an act (an act already outlined, indeed already accomplished before) of which it apparently has no trace. But in reality, if it recommences the outline for that act and believes it can do so with impunity (as does the fictitious character that it conceives for this purpose),[4] this is because the prior act was not sanctioned morally and consequently has to be put forth once more. For the soul has a secret but absolute need to have committed this act, and its conscience cannot be done with it until it assumes responsibility for it. Thus, even when Sade's atheist consciousness proclaims him irresponsible, his soul experiences only the more strongly the need to affirm itself in a guilty act.

This is why the same criminal situation that the dreamer imagines continues to be represented in his mind. Time empties the felonious acts of the past of their content and leaves the subsisting images of the things to which these acts refer. The image of things and of beings becomes a presence that provokes new acts, and the dreamer's project to perform them does not succeed in exhausting the provocation.

What is original in morose delectation in Sade is that it does not end in a literary composition. In lingering before the object of his exasperated virility, before the image of the virgin who makes this virility accursed, the Sadean soul will express a fear of losing itself as a consciousness, losing the very nucleus of its functions. But in tarrying before its object, exasperated virility recognizes and knows again only the same state of curse. The creative faculty that exasperation has developed in morose delectation is at bottom sterile; far from liberating, it welds new chains. This is why Sade transmits this morose delectation onto fictitious characters. In observing them, not only does he describe his own revery, he describes dreamers capable of realizing their dreams—or rather, his dreams. But to these dreamers who realize his dreams he necessarily gives his own psychological makeup, that of an insatiate dreamer deprived of any means of realizing his dreams except that of literary creation. Thus he shows them caught up in tireless recommencements; no successful enterprise ever satisfies them, nothing is ever done once and for all. This powerlessness to reach something that would be accomplished once and for all betrays the consciousness of the author. Not that the means of realization would have exempted Sade from writing: the realization, as he proved during his years of youth, always remained short of the conception, whatever would have been the means.

The characters Sade created translate the different forms of morose delectation, in particular that of expectation destructive of the present, into those disconcerting arguments without which they cannot give themselves over to their experimental debauchery. For them happiness consists not in gratification but in the desire to break the bonds that oppose desire. It is not in the presence of objects but in waiting for absent objects that those objects will be enjoyed. That is, their real presence will be enjoyed by destroying them (murders in debauchery). Or, if they are deceptive, apparently refusing to present themselves (in their resistance to what one would like to make them suffer), they will be mistreated so as to make them both present and destroyed. In some of Sade's characters deceived expectation ends by becoming an erotogenic fiction: no doubt the object is not deceptive, but it is treated as though it were. One of these characters, excessively favored by fortune, confesses that since he had only to wish in order to have, his pleasure has never been motivated by the objects that surround him, "but by what is not there." "Is it, as you say, possible to commit crimes as one conceives them? For my part, I confess that my imagination has always gone beyond my means: I have always conceived a thousand times more than I have done, and I have always complained that Nature gave me the desire to outrage her but always took from me the means to do so."

Here, too, Nature is experienced as a presence that escapes
the aggressive expectation of virility in a way no less exasperating
than the way virginal purity escapes accursed virility. Sade's consciousness sees itself faced with its own eternity, which it had disavowed and can now no longer recognize under the features of the
cunning Nature whose image it has conceived. Maintained in the
organic functions of its individual organism, the Sadean consciousness experiences its finiteness, but in the movements of its imagination it has a sensation of infinity. Instead of finding in that
sensation its eternal state and experiencing itself in a universal one-
ness, it perceives in that sensation as in a mirror the infinite reflection of the diverse and multiple possibilities lost for its soul. By
outraging God, it would cease to be a soul God has drawn from
nothingness and would return at once to all the eventualities that
nothingness contains prior to the soul's vocation, return to a
pseudoeternity, to the atemporal existence of perverse polymorphousness. Sade's characters, having disavowed the immortality of
the soul, now become candidates for integral monstrosity. Since
they disavow any (temporal) elaboration of their conscious personalities, their expectation paradoxically puts them back in the state
of possession of all the possibilities of a potential development of
those personalities. This state of possession is expressed in their
sentiment of unconditioned power.[5] The erotic imagination develops as the individual takes form by counterbalancing a perversion
with the instinct for propagation. This imagination chooses the moments in which the world and beings are absent and sinks its conscious personality into the solitude and expectation of soul of those
moments. It would then represent an attempt to recuperate all the
possible that has become impossible because the soul became conscious. For consciousness had constrained the soul to experience
the reality of the other, the possession and the loss of the other. In
its state of permanent expectation, Sade's soul gives itself over to
an imagination in which the soul decomposes, along with the object
it awaited, and returns to that atemporal state in which the posses-

sion of everything possible excluded the possibility of the painful experience of loss. Through the mouths of the characters he created, it is Sade himself who confesses: "I have invented horrors and carried them out in cold blood; since I had the resources to refuse myself nothing, however costly my projects for debauchery might be I set out on them at once." These words are Sade's own, for in fact the solitary one, the prisoner Sade, deprived of any means of action, in the end has at his command the same power as the omnipotent hero he dreams of: the unconditioned power that knows no obstacle either outside or within itself and that now feels only the blind flow of that power. "I set out on them at once," he says; this haste, however, hardly exhausts the movement of "that sort of inconstancy, scourge of the soul, and most distressing lot of our unhappy humanity." Sade's soul, aspiring to deliverance, is then exposed to a contradictory hope; it hopes to escape the painful experience of loss by refusing the object any presence, while in the very same moment it is dying with the desire to see the object, reestablished in the present, break in that soul the movement of time, which ruins it and exalts it over and beyond accursed virility.

APPENDIXES

Appendix 1

Who Is My Neighbor?

(*Esprit*, December 1938)

The general will, referring itself to the principles of universal reason, claims to eliminate the fluctuations of sense particulars. For every fluctuation of the human sensibility thereby reveals that was in error; every fluctuation of a particular sensibility reveals that it is itself error as such. The general will thus enables the majority, a mass, to be constituted into a sovereign people and to take itself to represent by itself the reasons the whole species has for existing. The general will thus rests on the misconception inherent to ethics that the individual could not by himself alone intrinsically represent the species. In this general will the only one that counts is he who reduces himself to a specific demand and can thus identify himself with other individuals who are likewise reduced to this demand. Logic then commands that we take the right to exist away from him who remains outside the species and is thus necessarily a monster. If it is true that "the Jacobins had all the virtues," civic virtue can be practiced only in conformity with the general will they incarnate, and pure and simple abstention will betray a vicious character in the abstainer. But the world of the general will, claiming to exclude the possibilities of error, also excludes the chances of sensibility. As these chances are the only ones worthy of the name, it excludes all chance in general. Those whom chance cannot favor will at least have the satisfaction of seeing chance no longer favor anyone. But then the relationship between the individual and popular sovereignty will henceforth be completely uncertain. Fraternity will no longer be experienced, because fraternity can be lived only in the fluctuations of sensibility, which, in the rule of abstract instances, are but the fluctuations of error. Among the just, not only is fraternity no longer manifest, but it disappears. There will be only individuals who are strangers for and indifferent to one another, individuals without obligation toward one another, so much so that they have to be bound together by contract. This is why, in the regime of the general will, a fraternal people is but a metaphor: even the majority that expresses itself by the general will is not a fraternal people. Though the practice of virtue is decreed in common, the possession of civic and moral qualities are not enough to establish bonds of fraternity or to produce an experience of such bonds. A fraternity that would be experienced requires an experienced bond of filiality that, common to all, attaches each to the same parental figure. It is, however, in the nature of an abstract instance that the only thing concrete in it is negation; its whole content will be a sensibility that, if it attempts anything, will attempt only to punish, will be wholly engaged in the punishing of a sensory particular. Popular sovereignty was born from parricide; its founding act is the putting to death of the king, a simulacrum of the murder of God. The revolutionary fraternity was then real inasmuch as it was sealed by the royal parricide. This is what the consciousness of the Marquis de Sade experienced so deeply when he demanded that the Republic resolutely consider itself to be in crime and assume authentic moral guilt instead of simply taking political responsibility for crime.

Appendix 2

The Father and Mother
in Sade's Work

Analytic psychology generally admits as a fact duly observed and beyond discussion that hatred of the father constitutes the initial conflict of most men. "It would be interesting to consider some exceptions; in some individuals there forms a conflict in the opposite direction." In Sade, "the principal events of his life seem to have singularly favored the more rare and generally less manifest complex of hatred of the mother. Traces of this are easily recognizable at every moment in his work; we can even consider it the constant theme of the Sadean ideology."[1] Must we trace Sade's psychic formation back to "a deception the mother would have inflicted on Sade when he was a child"? A traumatic moment motivated by real circumstances or due to an interpretation by the child, which would then have reinforced in the son a guilt feeling toward the father for having neglected the father too much?

In that case we would then find in Sade a negative Oedipus complex, brought about not, as in the case of a great number of neurotics, by the inhibition of incest due to castration anxiety, but by the regret for having wished to sacrifice the father to that false idol, the mother. Some homosexual neurotics, having given up on the conquest of the mother out of fear of the father, content themselves with adopting feminine behavior in their relationship with the father without daring to substitute themselves for him. Others turn their aggressivity, originally directed against the father, back against themselves and find themselves subject to the rigors of a superego of inexorable severity. Sade, for his part, allies himself with paternal power and, strong with his asocial superego, turns all his available aggressivity against the mother.

What are the reproaches that in the depths of his soul the young Sade addresses to his mother? Those he will later heap on his wife: *She is nothing but an impudent hussy.* He holds against her first of all her "female" egoism—he who will one day preach an anarchist philosophy. But in the course of his psychic evolution, all the motives for the hatred of his mother will become elements that Sade will exalt as attributes of paternal power. In the eyes of the son, the hypocrisy of the mother necessarily legitimates all the crimes of the father, who had been left aside. Then delinquency (evil) will be the repentant son's only means to pay his debt to the murderous, incestuous, and sodomist father.

Sade's "sadism" would then be the expression of a factor of primordial hatred that would have "chosen" the aggressive libido so as to be better able to carry out its mission—to chastise maternal power in all its forms and overthrow its institutions. At the end of an unbridled and already libertine adolescence, Sade sees standing before him, in the features of the President de Montreuil,[2] maternity jealous of its prerogatives, tyrannically disposing of her progeny as she will. Contact with his mother-in-law, this second mother, will make his aggressivity conscious and direct it into hatred of matriarchal values, into hatred of piety, beneficence, gratitude, sacrifice, and fidelity. Sade will set out to unveil "the self-interest and the fear that inspires them."

Sade's relationship with his wife will only reinforce this hatred. Knowing that she was not loved, she perhaps sought to impose herself on him through a devotion without bounds; Sade will resent it like a chain. He will see one purpose to this devotion: as Renée de Montreuil could not awaken love in him, she means at least to force him into gratitude in place of love. And so in all his writings he will continually criticize the feeling of gratitude. When Sade was a prisoner at Miolans, it was Renée alone who got him free; his detention was then extended at Vincennes, then in the Bastille, and only Renée's efforts could give him some hope. This dependence on a woman he did not love was intolerable to him, and in his works he will take vengeance for his inferiority. But little by little the feeling of dependence is generalized; Sade deepens it, extends it, so that finally it seems to him to be an original imperfection of the human race: "Women . . . are but a second means of Nature, one that deprives Nature from acting with her first means, a means therefore that inflicts outrage on her. . . . Nature would be well served if by exterminating all women, or by not ever willing to enjoy them, we would oblige Nature to resort to its first means to perpetuate the species." Is not this idea visibly inspired by revolt against an original gratitude, the gratitude man owes to the woman because he has come from her womb?

In other great figures of the preromantic period, the nostalgic desire to return to the serenity of the maternal bosom shows through in their vision of a golden age and of another world. But Sade seems to us to be constantly prey to an obsession with suffocation in the mother's womb. His acts and ideas are but the conscious manifestation of his struggle to extract his being from its original enclosure. Here is another reason for us to think that his long incarceration affected his person as the exteriorization of his obsession with the original imprisonment, and that in this way this period of detention contributed to make him take the peculiar attitude that he will then adopt toward society.

In *Justine, Juliette,* and *Philosophy in the Bedroom,* the mother always figures as a tyrannical idol, soon thrown from the altar on which social and religious veneration has put her and reduced, in the sadist sense of the word, to her condition of being the pleasure object of man. This conflict between the man and his mother will recur frequently in Sade's books. In *The Misfortunes of Virtue*, Bressac conceives a purely misogynous hatred for his mother: in the eyes of this sodomist, man is the only perfect specimen of the human race; women are but a deformation of men. His mother, an austere woman who wishes to lead him back to the good path, is in the eyes of the son but a pretext to thwart his life, and her morals appear to him as his worst enemy. Determined to get rid of her, he hopes to convince Justine to help him: " 'This being I am attacking,' he said, 'is the being that bore me in her womb. Is this vain consideration to stop me? On what grounds? Did this mother think of men when her lubricity made her conceive the fetus from which I derive? Can I owe her gratitude for having occupied herself with her own pleasure?' " Sade is so convinced of the judiciousness of this line of thought that he goes on to repeat Bressac's argument in all his other works. But, say the defenders of the matriarchal principle, does not the mother have the merit of having cared for her children? Sade foresees these objections and Bressac has his answer ready: " 'If our mother gave us good ways to carry on as soon as we were able to enjoy them,' he continues, 'we can love her, perhaps we even should do so. But if she gave us only bad ways to act, ways enjoined by no law of Nature, then not only do we owe her nothing, but everything dictates to us that we divest ourselves of them by that powerful force of egoism which naturally and invincibly commits man to get rid of all that harms him.' "

After the critique of the feeling of gratitude toward the mother, we have now a critique of the gratitude demanded for good acts, and a critique of beneficence, devotion, and sacrifice. Obsessed by his wife, Sade sets out to destroy the ideal of the devoted person. Justine only worsens her situation by seeking to obligate with her beneficence, precisely because she does good only "in order to tranquilize her conscience and for her own salvation." Not only do those who owe her some gratitude refuse it to her, but men like Dalville say they were wronged by having been obligated, for the necessity of being grateful is for them the most humiliating of states. Is Sade thinking of Renée's devotion and sacrifice when he makes Dalville say to Justine, after she has saved his life:

> What, I beg you, do you understand by this feeling of grati-
> tude with which you imagine you have captured me? . . .
> Reason better, wretched creature: what did you do when
> you aided me? Between the possibility of going your own
> way and coming to me, you chose the latter as a movement
> which your heart inspired in you. . . . You then gave your-
> self over to a pleasure? By what devil do you claim that I am
> obligated to recompense you for the pleasures you gave
> yourself?

Thus, to do good as to give birth to a child does would be nothing else than the result of an underlying satisfaction that one gives first to oneself. In Sade's eyes, maternal devotion, whether it comes from the spouse or the mother, is then but the maneuver of an egoism as monstrous as it is dissimulated.

The characteristic rivalry between a mother and her daughter cannot fail to be recorded in Sade's catalog. But this rivalry does not appear to him to be provoked so much by the desire to possess the father as by the desire to be freed by the father from the mater-nal duties that the mother transmits to her daughter. *Philosophy in the Bedroom* or *The Libertine Educators, Dialogues for Young Women,* which gives Sade's method for antimaternal education, shows us the mother chastised by the father in favor of the child.

With cruel joy Sade sets out to minutely describe scenes in which the mother is humiliated under the eyes of her children or by those children themselves. Was Sade thinking of his mother-in-law—whom he will nonetheless save from the scaffold—was he thus taking a more signal vengeance on the President by executing her in effigy and profaning the principles with which this authoritarian woman was imbued? Already in the character of Juliette, Sade had idealized the "tribade" woman (the woman without social commitment), setting her up against the social ideal of the mother. Dolmancé, the man who "never sleeps so soundly as when he has, during the day, sufficiently befouled himself with what our fools call crimes," expounds his conception of Nature, which brings out destruction and creation as but two aspects of one sole fundamental law. From this argument he will derive the final idea that murder is but a modification of the forms of matter. The argument will lead him to exalt tribadism, the sodomization of women, and pederasty. Dolmancé then contests the idea that procreation is a moral notion and attacks the paternal principle, the principle of social preservation.

How does it happen, one will ask, that there is nothing that speaks particularly of the hatred that Sade could have conceived for his own father, the instigator of his unhappy marriage? Let us leave to biographers the task of recognizing in the President de Blamont and his friend Olbourg, characters in *Aline and Valcour*, portraits of the Count de Sade and the President de Montreuil, and in their comings and goings and their way of disposing of their children for the purposes of debauchery a novelized caricature of the circumstances of Sade's marriage; it would be only to better avenge himself that he painted them in such black colors. Such vengeance does not exclude complicity. The fathers in *Aline and Valcour* and "Eugénie de Franval" are but variants of the character type that invariably reappears in the clandestine as well as in the signed works of the Marquis, a character type that Sade created for a great subversive mission: the father of the family who destroys his family. It is precisely in giving him the role of a black hero and not that of a virtuous and respectable man that Sade establishes between his own person and that of the father an identification that takes the form of a veritable adoration of the father. This adoration is the counterpart of the hatred dedicated to the mother, who always plays the role of honorable woman, so as to be more readily trampled underfoot.

"It is not the blood of the mother," says Bressac as he perpetrates his matricide, "that forms the child; it is that of the father alone. The female breast fructifies, preserves, builds up, but it provides nothing. This reflection would never make me cut short the days of my father, whereas I regard it as a quite simple matter to cut the thread of those of my mother." This anatomical conception, falsified perhaps deliberately, only shows us better to what extent Sade is obsessed by the necessity that requires man to be born of woman, which necessity appears to him to be a degradation both of Nature and of the human species. He then will depict for us the father as perpetually in revolt against the wife as a mother, who, everywhere in Sade's novels, is the obstacle to direct relations between the father and his children, and in particular to sodomist relations between father and son.

Sade exalts sodomy and incest as attributes of paternity; the father must break the conjugal chains that prevent him from enjoying his children physically. No natural law opposes this. Society has made certain natural laws into social laws; it has not legitimated others. This obliges Sadean fathers to resort to ruse, to hide their paternity from their daughters, in order to be able to possess them as they please once the daughters have reached the age of consent.

We could find no clearer example of the antimaternal complex than Bressac. Bressac has been orphaned of his father. But in the absence of a father, instead of transforming his state as a son into the role of second spouse of his mother (positive Oedipus complex), he to the contrary represents the natural virility and cruelty of the absent father; he as it were avenges that absence. Whereas in the Oedipus complex the suppression of the father makes possible the reestablishing of the primitive union of mother with child, here the suppression of the mother carried out conjointly by the father and the son (also recounted in the story of Brisa Tresta, in *Juliette*) brings out more clearly the latent rivalry between mother and son and reveals the community between son and father. In Sade's own case, the father chastising the mother in favor of the child, or breaking with his spouse out of love for the child, frees him from the maternal prison.

The underlying motive for the hatred of the mother (her imprisoning character is but a secondary elaboration) could well be closer to the resentment against the virgin than could be admitted. The virgin incarnating purity would originally be one with the mother idolized by the son. Then an event, or the simple suspicion of an event (suspicion constantly acts on Sade), makes the mother appear in a carnal aspect that inspires both attraction and repulsion. Has the adorable element betrayed? No, this adorable element retains all its intrinsic value, but it does not properly belong to the mother; it is the pure essence itself. Then for the image of the mother there is substituted that of the virgin.

But the psychoanalysts, who have to maintain the theory of the Oedipus complex, will say: this image retains the prohibiting Oedipal character of the mother. And they will add: it is because she is but variant and the Oedipal image of the mother that the virgin retains this character of excluding possession. The psychoanalysts see only a continuous genesis of motives; they are unable to admit the idea of a discontinuity of planes, which alone permits the soul to fix a value that would be irreducible. Without an irreducible value there is no conscience and no sublimation. But if the image of purity in its feminine aspect appeared to the child Sade first incarnated by his mother, it nonetheless exists independently in his mind as a quality subsequently identified with the objects of religion, and thus venerable—or blasphemable (as must be the case in Sade).

For Sade the mother holds the castrating role which in the Oedipus complex belongs to the father. She is the son's rival for the father (on the homosexual plane) as much as she is his rival for her daughter. Thus not only does the mother, stripped of any Oedipal attraction, represent imprisonment and suffocation (by social laws and by religion), but she loses the attraction of purity—a sacrilegious attraction that belongs to the religious and spiritual sphere and comes from a love transcended—in favor of the inaccessible virgin.

The initial event for Sade himself eludes our investigations. But it is reproduced in the circumstances of his marriage: his mother-in-law, the President de Montreuil, is substituted for his mother; he is himself inclined to the younger sister of the spouse imposed on him. For him, the incestuous situation takes form in this forbidden passion he will have for his sister-in-law. A key incident aggravates this situation: he takes his sister-in-law, a canoness, from her convent and makes her his mistress during his first trip to Italy. Sade cannot forget her even after several years of marriage. This results in the obstinately punitive action (Bastille, etc.) of the President de Montreuil, the prototype of the suffocating mother.

The image of the father destroyer of his own family here appears as a compensatory fable used by the atheistic consciousness of Sade's soul. It is through this phantasm that Sade leaves the maternal prison and can communicate with the essence of purity incarnate in the virgin; to the exclusionary character of the virgin Sade opposed the transgressing character of the father. The vocation of the virgin implies the renunciation of the maternal condition; it nonetheless also implies the creation of a carnal family, even in the name of a spiritual maternity. In Sade's mind, there is obviously no vocation that holds validity, but there does exist the for him ambiguous image of virginal purity. There is no question of renunciation either, but in an obsessive way this image of virginal purity, striking against virile possession, implies a prohibition of the family issued from carnal union. With these insinuating motifs, the phantasm of the father destroyer of his own family becomes as it were the sacrilegious context of inaccessible purity.

To conclude, I emphasize once again the Manichaean character of this personal mythology: the hatred of the mother and the hatred of matter are one and the same; the adoration of the destructive father also proceeds from the aspiration to destroy the original purity.

Appendix 3

The aspiration to integral monstrosity is in Sade the frenzied aspiration to try out all the imaginable forms of pleasure, to become the subject capable of exhausting the totality of the possible (whereas this totality of the possible can never be attained, the possible in fact being what is impossible to exhaust, being the inexhaustible). How can we not compare it with the heretical doctrine of Carpocrates, the Gnostic sectarian whose aspiration to original purity by way of a practice exhausting all crimes throws a revealing light on the organization of a mind such as the one we are studying?

> Agree with thine adversary quickly, whilst thou are in the
> way with him; lest at any time the adversary deliver thee to
> the judge, and the judge deliver thee to the officer, and
> thou be cast into prison. Verily I say unto thee, thou shalt
> by no means come out thence, till thou has paid the utter-
> most farthing. (Matthew 5:25–26)

The Carpocratian sect gave this passage a deep interpretation; they saw in it the confirmation of their doctrine of nonresistance to the creator of this world of darkness, from which Jesus has come to deliver man, to restore him to the light of the heavenly Father. According to them, the omission of sins brings about the reincarnation of the soul, required by the creator of this world, until that soul has consummated all its guilt. Crime is a tribute paid to life, they say, a tribute demanded by the creator of this life. It is necessary, then, that the soul deliver itself over to sin as soon as temptation presents itself, lest it be delivered over to the judge (the evil God, creator of this world) who will cast it into prison—into a new body—until it has paid all its debts, to the uttermost farthing. For them, the Gospel teaches men how one has to render to the light what belongs to the light by giving to darkness what belongs to darkness. The myth of the reincarnation of the soul, common to all the Gnostics, presupposes a quantitative conception of the integral soul; successive reincarnations exhaust its guilt.

The reason for this is that the Carpocratians did not wish to recognize in Jesus the Man-God whose Incarnation came to assume all guilt and to suppress every necessity for a reincarnation of the soul, in the Carpocratian sense—or every reiteration of the transgressing act, in Sade's sense. As soon as one rejects the representations of God incarnated once and for all in man, the idea of a reincarnation in order to exhaust what sins remain to be committed, or the need to recommence sin indefinitely, or the necessity of the eternal return of the Same, which, according to Nietzsche, makes the soul go through a series of diverse existences and identities before returning to a first conscious identity—present themselves to thought as so many economies of Being.

Notes

Translator's Introduction

[1] Various essays published from 1933 on were reworked and collected in *Sade My Neighbor,* published in 1947. "The Philosopher-Villain" was first given as a lecture in the Tel Quel forum and then added to the 1967 edition of *Sade My Neighbor.* It was also published in vol. 16 of the *Oeuvres complètes* of the Marquis de Sade (Paris: Cercle du Livre Précieux, 1967).

Preface

[1] The author will deal with this theme much later, but *in su loco proprio,* in *Le bain de Diane.*

The Philosopher-Villain

[1] Elaborations, and digressions, on a paper entitled "Sign and Perversion in Sade" read to Tel Quel on 12 May 1966.

[2] See "Note concerning My Detention" in Marquis de Sade, *Cahiers personnels (1803–1804),* unpublished texts edited, with preface and notes, by Gilbert Lély (Paris: Corréâ, 1953). [English translation in Marquis de Sade, *The Complete Justine, Philosophy in the Bedroom, and Other Writings,* trans. Richard Seaver and Austryn Wainhouse (New York: Grove Press, 1965), p. 153. Throughout, all citations to published English-language

editions of the Marquis de Sade's works have been added by the trans-
lator.]

[3] Marquis de Sade, *Juliette*, trans. Austryn Wainhouse (New York:
Grove Press, 1976), p. 450.

Sade My Neighbor

Sade and the Revolution

[1] See Appendix 1.

[2] Marquis de Sade, *Philosophy in the Bedroom*, in *The Complete Justine,
Philosophy in the Bedroom, and Other Writings*, p. 333. Further citations to
Philosophy in the Bedroom are given in the text using the abbreviation *PB*.

[3] This passage, as well as the following one, gives evidence of the ten-
dentious deviation of the author's reasoning at the time he composed this
study. What the "utopia of evil" leaves out of account is not ennui but the
functional, or utilitarian, character that the institutions of a given social
milieu give to the exercise of impulsive forces. If there is here a question of
a utopia of "evil," it is because Sade, using the language of institutions,
sketches out the idea of a human grouping that would declare itself to be
in "permanent insurrection" because of the "state of perpetual motion"
of its members, one that would have become conscious of being founded
on nothing else but the exercise of impulses freed from every ideological
legitimation. As a result, the behavior of individuals as well as the nature of
their actions would be changed; this is what makes Sade's project utopian.
For if disgust and ennui follow "crime committed solely for the sake of
committing a crime," it is only in the existing institutional world that there
arises the idea of such a crime, followed by ennui or a fall in intensity. The
functional tendency of institutionally structured impulses is so strong that
the individual never, or very rarely, succeeds in maintaining himself at the
level of an impulsive intensity as soon as the impulse ceases to respond as a
means to the goal assigned by the institutions—in general, the goal of their
conservation, a transcendental signification, the Good of all. The real
problem would instead be to know what in the state of "permanent insurrection" would still structure the impulsive forces, and in what acts these
forces would be recognized to have no other end but themselves.

Outline of Sade's System

[1] See the biography, unequaled to this day, of Gilbert Lély, *Vie du marquis de Sade* (Paris: Jean-Jacques Pauvert, 1965).

[2] Marquis de Sade, *Dialogue entre un prêtre et un moribund*, published for the first time in conformity with the unpublished signed manuscript, with preface and notes, by Maurice Heine (Paris: Stendhal, 1926). [Quotations from the English translation by Austryn Wainhouse, *Dialogue between a Priest and a Dying Man*, in *The Complete Justine, Philosophy in the Bedroom, and Other Writings*, pp. 168–69. Further citations to this work are in the text.]

[3] Marquis de Sade, *Les infortunes de la vertu*, text verified with the original signed manuscript and published for the first time with an introduction by Maurice Heine (Paris: Éditions Fourcade, 1930), Introduction, pp. xxxviii–xxxix.

[4] Marquis de Sade, *Justine*, in *The Complete Justine, Philosophy in the Bedroom, and Other Writings*, p. 742.

[5] Marquis de Sade, *Les 120 journées de Sodome ou l'École du libertinage*, critical edition established on the basis of the original autograph manuscript by Maurice Heine, vol. 1 (Paris: Stendhal, 1931). [English translation by Austryn Wainhouse and Richard Seaver, *The 120 Days of Sodom* (New York: Grove Press, 1966).]

[6] Marquis de Sade, *La Nouvelle Justine ou les malheurs de la vertu*, followed by *Histoire de Juliette sa soeur*, 10 vols. (Holland, 1797). This edition containing the second version of *Juliette* is the third version of *Justine*. [Marquis de Sade, *Justine*, trans. Austryn Wainhouse (New York: Grove Press, 1978); *Juliette*, trans. Wainhouse (Grove Press, 1976).]

[7] See *Justine*, p. 52; see also *Philosophy in the Bedroom*.

[8] *The 120 Days of Sodom*, p. 253.

[9] Marquis de Sade, *Juliette*, trans. Austryn Wainhouse (New York: Grove Press, 1968), p. 399; henceforth cited in the text as *J*.

[10] Not only does Sade speak as a precursor of evolutionism, but he here puts forth an idea that corresponds to certain present-day conceptions of the past and present faculties of Nature for the production of species: is man really a termination?

[11] In this Sadean perspective of an original eternal Nature existing independently of its creatures, and in particular of man, it would be interesting to pursue the prolongations of Spinoza's "atheist" doctrine of "Deus sive Natura"—"Deus" being interpreted as a rhetorical precaution. This interpretation makes us understand why, in the first part of *Juliette*, Dalbène

recommends that Juliette read the author of the *Ethics,* likening him to Vanini and d'Holbach: "Nourish yourself with the great principles of Spinoza. . . . " Compare Sade's discussion of Nature with some of Spinoza's propositions: "As he exists for the sake of no end, he also acts for the sake of no end. Rather, as he has no principle or end of existing, so he also has none of acting. What is called a final cause is nothing but a human appetite insofar as it is considered as a principle, *or* primary cause, of some thing." [Benedict Spinoza, *Ethics,* 4, Preface, in *The Collected Works of Spinoza,* ed. and trans. Edwin Curley (Princeton, N.J.: Princeton University Press, 1985), p. 544.] "All final causes are nothing but human fictions" [ibid., 1, Appendix, p. 442]. "From this it follows also that God does not give man laws in order to reward him when he fulfills them. To put it more clearly, God's laws are not of such a nature that they could ever be transgressed. For the rules that God has established in Nature, according to which all things come to be and endure—if we want to call them laws—are such that they can never be transgressed. E.g., *that the weakest must yield to the strongest, that no cause can produce more than it has in itself,* etc., are of such a kind that they never change, never begin, but that everything is disposed and ordered under them. To say something about them briefly, all laws that cannot be transgressed are divine laws. For whatever happens is, not contrary to, but according to his own decree. All laws that can be transgressed are human laws. For everything that man decides for his own well-being is not necessarily for the well-being of the whole of Nature also. On the contrary, it may be destructive of many other things." "So also man, as a particular thing, has no further purpose than his limited essence can attain; but as a part and instrument of the whole of Nature, this end of his cannot be the ultimate end of Nature, because it is infinite and must use man along with all other things, as its instrument." [*Short Treatise on God, Man, and His Well-Being,* 2, chap. 24, in *The Collected Works of Spinoza,* pp. 142–43.]

[12] *Justine,* p. 81.

[13] *Philosophy in the Bedroom.*

Under the Mask of Atheism

[1] In fact, courtly love is not so much concerned with the "virgin" as with the "woman of one's thoughts," with the woman inaccessible because married to one's suzerain, or the "Queen," who, like the "virgin," has the character of being a forbidden object but is generally the object of an adul-

terous passion that then spiritualizes itself. In Sade, who was familiar with the Provençal tradition of courtly love, we find the strange relationship he maintains with the shadow of his ancestor Laure de Sade, celebrated by Petrarch, who had become for Sade a tutelary figure. See Sade's letter to his wife dated 1781, written in the donjon of Vincennes, in which he recounts the dream in which Laure appeared to him and expressed her compassion for her great-great-nephew.

[2] Whence those prodigious stagings in *The Story of Justine and Juliette,* which he composes during the years of the Directorate to compensate for the loss of his manuscript of *The 120 Days of Sodom,* which he will not be able to recover. This loss was consequential for all his activity between his imprisonment in the Bastille and his final internment in Charenton. At the beginning, *Justine* had the dimensions only of a short story, entitled *The Misfortunes of Virtue,* in which the heroine bears the revealing name of Sophie. This short story was composed in the Bastille at the same time as the tales of *Crimes of Love,* on the margin of the great systematic work which *The 120 Days of Sodom* constituted for the author. Of his works of lesser dimensions, it was *The Misfortunes of Virtue* that seems to have appeared in the eyes of the Marquis most apt to fill the void left by the disappearance of *The 120 Days,* whether because the plot of the story of the two sisters allowed him to restore a gallery of clinical portraits, or because the theme of this story and the lesson that emerges therefrom throw a metaphysical light on the sometimes strictly documentary scenes of the chronicle of the Chateau of Silling. The result was that *The Misfortunes* will develop into the ten volumes of *The Story of Justine and Juliette.* Thus, in the absence of the *120 Days,* this work will constitute the clandestine summa of Sade's thought, presented anonymously to a public traumatized by the Terror, a public that longs to evacuate the effects of the Terror in readings that enable it to master its emotions and to "benefit" from them. . . . In the *Crimes of Love,* however, this same thought, as it were divorced from itself, sets out to normalize its most imperious motifs. This effort, which borrows criteria that, in the eyes of the author as well as in those of the tradition, should be taken with reservations, in reality scarcely legitimates itself except by the need to communicate. It thus puts before us the problem, what exactly is the function of the public work alongside the clandestine work if it is not simply a screen hiding it? Despite the means used, despite the flagrant duplicity, would there not be a profound aspiration to put oneself in the full light not of society but of judgment? Would there not be an obscure avowal of dissatisfaction left by the clandestine expression?

[3] "The Latins derived *morosus* from *mos,* custom, and from *mora,* delay,

from which the French obtained *demeurer*, from *demorari*. As customs appear alien from one people to another, one province to another, and as delay brings on disquietude and impatience, our word means strange, singular, bizarre, and, on the other hand, troubled, sad, unquiet. The following verse line expresses both this twofold origin and this double meaning:

mos me morosum, mora me facit esse morosum.

"Our French language has conserved in *morose* the secondary meaning of *mora*, which makes the word mean sad, mournful, somber.

"Theologians, who have a language particular to themselves, have adopted the primitive meaning of *mora*; they use *morose* to characterize things that remain for a time; a morose delectation is for them a delectation that lasts for some time." M. Lachort, *Somme théologique de saint Thomas* (Paris: Vives, 1863), vol. 5, p. 70.

[4] It matters little whether it is a matter of a project that was not realized or of an act that was performed; before God the soul remains no less responsible for projects to which its will has given its attention (the sin of morose delectation consists precisely in this) as for the realization in acts that this will commands.

[5] See Appendix 3.

Appendixes

[1] For documentation, I here reproduce some extracts from my article entitled "Éléments d'une étude psychanalytique sur le Marquis de Sade," *Revue de psychanalyse* 6, nos. 3–4 (1933).

[2] With the formidable means in her power, she will persecute him to the point of reducing him to impotence.